Escape From Hell to Heaven

By Cornell Iliescu
With Helen Nielsen

Escape From Hell to Heaven
© 2022 Cornell Iliescu
All rights reserved

First edition printed **Dec**ember 2022
Published by Solutions Press

All rights reserved. Except as permitted by applicable copyright laws, no part of this book may be reproduced, duplicated, sold, or distributed in any form or by any means, either mechanical, by photocopy, electronic, or by computer, or stored in a database or retrieval system, without the express written permission of the publisher or author, except for brief quotations by reviewers.

ISBN: 979-8-9864517-3-2

Printed in the United States of America

This is a work of non-fiction.
The ideas and stories presented are those of the author alone.

Front Cover Photo

Cornell Iliescu with the 1939 Buick his father drove to rescue downed airmen in 1943 in Romania. It was later smuggled out of Romania. Cornell found the car in 2006 and purchased it on Ebay. He has shown the car in numerous parades and car shows. Photo by Rick Rosen, photographer, Newport Berach, California

Back Cover Photo

The American bomber *The Sandman*, piloted by Bob Sternfels, attacking the Ploesti oil refineries that Cornell witnessed August 1, 1943.

Table of Contents

Acknowledgements v
Dedication viii
Introduction xii
Chapter One: The War Years 1
My Family Before the War 6
Chapter Two: The Aftermath 7
Chapter Three: Survival 13
Chapter Four: The Americans 15
Chapter Five: Growing Up 21
Chapter Six: My Military Experience 23
Chapter Seven: A Lucky Break 27
Chapter Eight: Coming Home 33
Chapter Nine: Music in my Life 35
Chapter Ten: I get Married 37
Chapter Eleven: A Better Position 39
Chapter Twelve: Music 45
Chapter Thirteen: The Relationship 51
Chapter Fourteen: My Livelihood 55
Chapter Fifteen: Sincron and My Escape 59
Chapter Sixteen: On our Way to Freedom 73
Chapter Seventeen: Touchdown on US Soil 81
Chapter Eighteen: The Divorce bombshell 105
Chapter Nineteen: Dreams to Come 109

Acknowledgements

Helen Nielsen

Soon after meeting Helen in 2002, I felt the time had come to put my dreams and goals into action. I wanted to dedicate my life to helping the American Veterans and ultimately build a memorial to the young American fliers who were missing in action over my country. This was something about which I was an eyewitness as a child. It was I who came up with the name of The Noble Cause Foundation and together we visited the attorney to draw up the papers for a non-profit corporation. We also worked on the By-Laws and after that we started writing this book.

The process was that I would write my thoughts about my life story in both Romanian and English when at home. Then we would get together and work it out so that the written words described exactly what I wanted to say in the way that I wanted to say it. This worked out well for us.

Cornell Iliescu

Lee Pound

He was referred to us as an excellent author, editor, and publisher. He came to the rescue and did such a superb job of editing and preparing the book for publication, that we owe it to him that this book ever came to be. He made it happen!

Thank you, Lee.

Gerry Rubin

Owner of Sitelines Productions, Inc. an integrated Experience Design and Production company in Costa Mesa, CA. Since the mid-nineties, Gerry showed great interest in my restoration of vintage military vehicles and later caught the spark of what we were planning to do in the future. He has been a huge supporter who has helped me in so many ways, from creating a concept for the future WWII memorial, to allowing me to use his museum for Patriotic Events and as a home base for the Noble Cause Foundation. Gerry is a true Patriot!

I would also like to thank all those who supported the Noble Cause Foundation in a big or small way.

Victor Bakkila, Police Captain at the City of Costa Mesa, Jack Hammett, Bill Mimiaga, Dennis Leslie, Fred McDowell, Peter Zappas, Wendy Leece. Pat Nangle, David Champlin, Vince Weatherby, Kimberly Yaeger Lacy, Steve and Linda Cochrum, Caley Carr, Tony Mercuro, Elizabeth Parker, Ron Bitzer, Matthew Caffrey, Donovan Sinohue, Debbie and Luis Alva, Rick Goldsmith, Mauro Nicola, Jeff Willis, Pete Peterson, Tony Roman, Emma Clark, Chris Schneer, Carolyn Ross, Gina Salvaggi, Jeanne Koelsch, and the Danciu family. The Harmonettes from Vista, CA, namely, Sheryl Goodman, Maureen Mullins, and Lisa Hightower, made every event special with their portrayal of the Andrews Sisters from WWII, and brought big band era nostalgia.

Our dear friend, Nicholas Dimancescu, the young documentary director, had it in his plans to make a short documentary about my story. His life was cut short, at 26, when he fell to his death while catching a special shot when filming in the Carpathian Mountains of Romania.

When I first danced with Pat, I realized that I had found the dance partner that I had been looking for.

Here we are dancing in Garden Grove at the Classic Car Show. It was my 82nd birthday.

Dedication

This book is dedicated to my father and my hero, Emil Iliescu, who made the choice to risk his own life to save the lives of the young American fliers in burning planes who crash landed during WWII.

He inspired me to continue his legacy.

Citizens around Orange County Paid solemn homage to the U.S. men and women who have died serving their country. Here are a few of the ways they observed Memorial Day on Monday, May 9, 2017.

(From The Orange County Register)

Sage Iliescu is shown how to salute by his grandfather Cornell Iliescu before the 63rd Annual Memorial Day Service at Harbor Lawn-Mount Olive Memorial Park on Monday, May 29, 2017 in Costa Mesa, California. (Photo by Josh Barber)

Sage, age ten, playing taps on Memorial Day 2017

I want to acknowledge my grandson, Sage Iliescu, who at the early age of 10 years, had the talent and the courage to play Taps at the Memorial Day Ceremony at Mt. Olive-Harbor Lawn Cemetery in Costa Mesa in front of more than 500 people! He has continued to be a part of my Patriotic Events ever since. Your grandpa is proud of you!

Introduction

On August 1, 1943, 178 B-24 Liberators left Benghazi Air Base in northern Africa on a mission to bomb the oil refineries near Ploesti, Romania. Operation Tidal Wave, a daring, low-level raid, cost the lives of over 300 crewmen and the loss of 58 aircraft. The raid reduced the total refining capacity of the six targets by forty-six percent. The defending forces, unfortunately, were alerted in advance and were waiting for the approaching bombers.

Anti-aircraft crews fired machine guns and small firearms at point blank range, setting up a virtual wall of deadly fire. The Americans ignored the obvious danger and pressed home the attack despite fierce opposition. The President awarded no less than five Congressional Medals of Honor for heroic action on that mission, some posthumously.

On the ground, in the little village of Snagov, about 29 miles from the capital of Bucharest and about 13 miles from Ploesti, lived a small boy, the son of the foreman of the automotive fleet of the Concordia-Vega Refinery, one of the targets assigned to the 93rd Bomb Group. It sustained minor damage that day but left the boy with vivid memories of standing on the roof of his house watching planes, explosions, fires, and dense black smoke cover the area.

Because of the strategic importance of cutting Germany's oil supply, the allies hit Ploesti many times during the war. That small boy, Cornell Iliescu, still remembers another bombing raid that occurred many months later. Here is his story.

Chapter One:
The War Years

In 1942 I was almost 4 years old, and my brother was 10. We lived in the capital city of Bucharest at the headquarters of the Concordia-Vega Oil Refinery. The company allowed only a few employees to live inside the compound, my father among them. We lived in a two-story beige brick building of nice architectural design. I believe the building where we lived is still there today.

When the war started, my dad thought it would no longer be safe for us to continue to live in Bucharest near the refinery because of past bombing raids at the railroad marshalling yards and at other important factories.

Every time the bombing raids started, every building in the city sounded its sirens. My dad realized that getting to the bunkers every time an air raid happened created a dangerous, impossible situation. Worse than that, on many occasions by the time we reached the bunkers the doors had closed. We tried to communicate with the people inside to open the doors. I remember my mother banging on the door with a heavy piece of metal to make the people inside hear us and let us in. This frequently happened during the night. Most of the time my dad wasn't there. We couldn't use any type of lamp or flashlight. Trying to get two small children out of bed, down several stories of our building, and out through the compound to the bunker created a hair-raising experience. Nobody designed the bunker, the basement of a large four-story building, to survive bombing raids. After a few incidents like that, my father arranged with his boss to move our family near to where he lived, about 29 miles from the capital and about 13 miles from the Ploesti Oilfields.

This small village, Snagov, was a resort area with a lake and lavish summer villas. My dad rented a two-bedroom house across the street from where his boss lived so he could be reached in the event of an emergency on a 24-hour basis. In the backyard of that house the Romanian Army operated a radio station where they monitored the air raids headed toward Ploesti. The Romanian soldiers, for their own protection, dug a large trench where they sought refuge in case the bombing raids came too close. They often jumped into the trench to seek cover. They allowed us to use the trench, too.

This an oxygen tank like the ones dropped into Lake Snagov and collected by my brother.

As a very young child, I stayed close to my mother, but she had a difficult time with my brother. He never joined us in the trench and later

The War Years

when my mother looked for him, she'd find him in the tallest cherry tree, where he watched the bombers and the dogfights, a stressful situation for her. One day during a dogfight, the rapid fire of a machine gun cut through the branch where he sat. He fell to the ground. It scared the heck out of him but took care of the problem. He came home screaming. After that he never went up the tree again.

As a child, I didn't fully understand the events happening around me. My safety and security lay with my mother and father. My brother, being older than I by six years, spent much of his time with my Uncle Stefan. He often went with my father's brother into the Snagov Lake, where he swam around and gathered up the oxygen tanks dropped by the American planes. My dad later adapted them to carry wine because the metal was pure and safe to use.

Lake Snagov Summer 1943 brother John, father Emil, uncle Stefan, and Cornell

Every time a dogfight took place nearby, my mother rushed with me into the deep trench to protect us from flying shrapnel. Many times, I watched the sky   and saw that with so much fire going on a parachute coming out of a bomber was lucky to not catch on fire. I recall my mother covering my face so I couldn't see what happened in sky, especially when some parachutes caught on fire on their way down or when enemy fire hit them before they touched the ground. The chaos was beyond belief. The exploding bombs and the frightening roar of the planes spinning down and out of control before they crash landed looked like the end of the world. Many times, the planes came apart as they descended in a ball of fire. Everything seemed to take a long time, yet probably took not more than an hour. It seemed as if it happened in slow motion.

On the following day, after the bombing raids stopped, my dad came home to check on his family. While my mother fixed dinner, he sat at the table and told my mother stories about trying to save the lives of those in the downed B-24s and B-17s and about how many times the bodies were burned beyond recognition. He saved a lot of lives but some of them weren't so lucky. The ones who survived often gave him an article of clothing as a memento, a thank you for saving their lives and for helping them by making sure they made it to the Romanian authorities for food and medical assistance. I remember some boots, trousers, and bomber jackets. One time he brought home some sticks of chewing gum, a first for all of us, something we had never tried or even heard of before.

We lived in the village of Snagov for approximately three years until the war ended

My Family Before the War

Top Left: My cousins Pepi and Christina and brother John in summer of 1939
Top Right: My mother and myself, spring 1939, Bucharest
Bottom Left, My dad, Elim Iliescu in Central Park Bucharest September 1942
Bottom Right: Cornell age 6 and mother Mary with dog Lucky in Snagov during 1944 Ploesti bombing raids

Chapter Two:
The Aftermath

When the end of the war approached, the Russians began invading Romania. I was unaware of everything that happened, but it seems like only yesterday when my mother gave me a bath indoors while I stood up in a washtub. She poured water from a small tin cup and told me how the Bolsheviks were invading our country, that we lost the war and along with that, our freedom.

To a 6-year-old boy the name Bolshevik seemed like a funny, yet scary name. I pictured them as monsters ready to eat us up.

My parents talked every day about the arrival of the Bolsheviks. When the time came close, the government called our soldiers back to their units and we never saw them again. We bought food from the people in the village who raised animals and other food. We heard about how they, too, were afraid and concerned about what would happen to them when the Russians arrived in the village.

Not long after that, the Russians came on horseback, in trucks, and wagons, some driven by women, through our little village. Thousands of them. They searched every house as they entered our village and ordered everyone to go to their front yards. When they got to our home, we too got out of the house and onto the front porch. My father was at work. My mother held me in her arms. My brother stood beside us. We were very frightened but tried to be quiet and comply with their orders.

While we stood on the porch, they ordered my aunt, in her twenties, to go inside. While she was in the house, one of the soldiers put his rifle to my throat and said, "If you don't obey their orders and be quiet, we'll blow your head off."

I remember my aunt's screams to this day. My mother was so scared that she collapsed to the floor with me in her arms, almost kissing the soldier's boots, and begged him not to hurt me. After they raped my aunt, the soldiers left. My mother couldn't utter a word for hours.

More soldiers passed through. A Romanian interpreter, a soldier, and a drunken Russian sergeant explained that they were looking for alcohol and weren't interested in our story of rape.

Now I realize that in my small boy mind the idea of monsters wasn't far from the truth. I never knew the rifle pointed into my neck could kill me. The rifle didn't make me cry. It was my yelling and screaming aunt, who was with four soldiers. Days went by filled with anxiety. Our worries grew greater day by day. Survival became my parents' number one concern.

In the mind of a small boy, the contrasting images of the American Airmen who offered me chocolates, big smiles, and kind words and of the harsh Russian soldiers with their loud voices, mean faces, and violent actions stayed with me for many years to come and changed me forever.

The time came for us to return home to the capital, Bucharest, from the village of Snagov where we spent the war.

In Bucharest my dad worked at the Concordia-Vega refinery, which was destroyed during the war. He was worried

The Aftermath

about his job and how he would support his family when everything, especially food, was hard to come by.

So, he put his family in a horse-drawn cart with a few belongings and sent us 29 miles back home.

I remember that during the war I made two good friends, the first a male tiger cat named Pisu, a very loyal cat. He caught mice or rats and put them in the front entrance on the doormat to show how hard he worked for his food. I could not leave him behind.

My second friend was a rooster named Coco. During the war whenever my dad came home, Coco flew up to his shoulder and loved to eat from the palm of his hand. He also came along in the same wagon with me. He never left my side during the entire journey home, which took a very long time.

After many hours of travel, we entered downtown Bucharest. It looked like a scene from the apocalypse. Buildings smashed into rubble, a sad sight. Many times, we turned to take other streets because the rubble and bricks covered the road. The city looked like this for quite a few years. The German Luftwaffe, before they surrendered, pounded the capital with bombs to punish the Romanians for switching sides to the Allies. The people paid dearly for this.

Our driver drove around massive piles of rubble in the middle of the streets until we managed to get home. My brother jumped out of the cart to help guide us to our house, near the headquarters of Concordia-Vega Oil Refinery, where my parents lived from 1937 to 1952. Suddenly our building appeared, standing alone among the remains of buildings that no longer existed.

Across from our building, the building where my friend lived was gone. I asked my mother what she thought had happened to my friend Dan. She said she hoped they had enough time to make it to a bunker across the way.

In front of our building, a lot of poor looking people stood in a long line to pick up food stamps for bread. Lines stretched everywhere, every couple of blocks. Hundreds of people, including children, waited for food. It didn't matter whether you were 6 or 86, you still waited in endlessly long lines. One day when I carried soup home, I spilled some on my legs. Not only was it hot but every drop was precious.

As soon as we pulled into the driveway of the company headquarters, my two loyal buddies, my pets Pisu and Coco, immediately started checking around to get used to this new home. Coco landed on the top of the woodpile in the yard and wandered around as if he owned the place. Pisu seemed to recognize his long ago home and waited by the entrance for someone to let him in. We carried our meager belongings into the house. The food we brought with us spoiled from the heat of the long journey.

My mother looked around and couldn't believe that next door to us, almost wall to wall, sat an unexploded 250-pound bomb. The army came to defuse the bomb but because of its weight, they needed special equipment, a crane, to get it out through the roof.

After so many years away, I was able to take a bath in a tub. We started as best we could to live again like human beings.

The next morning, I went out to see if I could find my friend Dan but saw no sign of him. Instead, quite a few soldiers and amputees in flatbed trailers played accordions and waited for people to give them a few pennies. That was my first impression after the war and how things were now. Many people were gone and never came back home. On every corner

The Aftermath

near my house people sat on their luggage with no place to go. The government could not control the turmoil. Everywhere Russian tanks and troops gave orders and scared people. Day by day, as I learned more about the crisis in my country, I was always afraid, especially since my parents seemed afraid, too.

It didn't take too long before my brother of fourteen met some new and old friends. They talked about a new movie playing down the street starring Gary Cooper. Being older, he didn't like being a babysitter, but he knew I liked cowboy movies. We knew this type of movie would soon be gone.

One day in the summer of 1946, my brother told me about a great new movie, but it was not about cowboys. He asked if I would like to see it. Though only 8 at the time I'd never refuse to see an American movie. To this day I never regret seeing that movie, *Sun Valley Serenade* with John Payne and Sonja Henie. The biggest star for me in that movie was a person who remained my idol for the rest of my life, Glenn Miller. The excitement of his music, such as *In the Mood* and *Chattanooga Choo Choo,* has stayed with me since then.

The most important part of the story, which inspired my brother and me, showed us a way for us to go to America. We learned how Sonja Henie in the story was an orphan and through the help of the Red Cross obtained a sponsor and went to America.

Later we found out about Red Cross offices where you could register as an orphan if you were accompanied by an adult. My brother applied and they believed him but when they saw me, they sent me home to my mother since I looked well cared for. My bother was very convincing, and he and his two friends made it as far as customs at the ship. When they presented their papers to be processed before boarding, they were interrogated by some Red Cross officials and denied departure. For two days my parents never heard from him, and they were sick with worry, but I was happy for him thinking he had made it and soon I would receive a letter from America.

Chapter Three: Survival

Every day the country changed dramatically in many ways. Survival was still the number one priority. Our new friends or neighbors were not the same as our old ones, who you could relate to and grow close to socially. Now you know to never trust them. They might turn you in for favors from the local officials to make their lives easier. You never knew what you did or said might be the reason. Just being suspect was reason enough. Not only was daily life difficult but this lack of friendship among neighbors made everything more desperate and colder.

Every day my father came home he told us another friend or associate was missing from the job and their family would have no right to ask when or where they might see him again. This became our way of life for many years to come.

I remember one day when two men with hats and long coats knocked on our door and asked to search the house for any documents, newspapers, or magazines. They even checked our schoolbooks to see if we had ripped the picture of King Michael from the front as required. I remember the day when the teacher told me to rip it out. I cried all day and refused to tear the page. I learned later that my mother found our books and removed all the pictures. It was lucky she did that because any materials found that linked us to organizations not approved of by the new Communist regime would give them reason to take my parents away from us for the rest of our lives. My parents were smart enough to see in advance that this could happen and burned everything like that.

After they finished the search, they wrote out a receipt for the radio they found and told my mother that the radio was being confiscated until the new government took over. She would be notified when she could pick up the radio. Two years later we got it back.

Soon the government changed the way we addressed each other in the Romanian language. We could no longer address anybody in any polite way except with the Russian word, Tovarich, which means Comrade. We were told that we could no longer say Mister and Missus because Mister and Missus were now in jail, and we were all equal. Even our street names were changed to Russian names. It took us years to figure out how to get around. They removed many school subjects such as foreign languages and made it mandatory to learn Russian. As soon as our king abdicated all American movies disappeared and the only movies in the theatre were about the glory of the Russian army during World War II.

Chapter Four:
The Americans

When the time came for me to change from elementary school to the next level, I had to take a different direction to school and remember like yesterday the pain of missing an event I loved dearly.

On the way to elementary school, I passed the American Embassy. Every morning at five minutes to eight I watched a US Marine run the American flag up the flagpole and give a snappy salute. I was so impressed watching him do this each day that I never thought much about my freezing toes where my mother had cut off the end of my shoes so they would fit my growing feet. Years after, during summer vacation, I rose early just to see the flag raising. Something about those colors stirred my soul and brought me back to the moment when I first saw them.

Back in August 1944 my dad and I drove back to the small village of Snagov, where we lived as refugees during the war. My dad spotted a low flying B 24 Liberator that seemed like it might crash land in front of us. As it descended, it veered toward a cornfield alongside the highway. Soon after, the plane crash landed, but without an explosion or fire. My father jumped out of the car and ran to see what happened. I followed. When we reached the plane, I walked near the collapsed wing, but my father told me to stand back because the plane could blow up at any minute. Dust and the smell of fuel permeated everywhere, but my dad proceeded anyway to see what could be done. He ripped off what was left of the bomb bay door to get access to the smoking bomber. He pulled three aviators from the wreckage and laid their semiconscious bodies nearby in the dirt. At the same time, he was aware that at any moment the German or Romanian Military Police would arrive at the crash site. He carried them to his car. From there he drove them to a wooded area near the railroad tracks, which hid them from view.

My father told me to stay with them until he returned. He also said that if he didn't come back soon, I needed to get my Uncle Stefan, who lived close by, to bring a cart to take the wounded to the infirmary.

B-24 Bomber, presumed to be the one that Emil Iliescu helped the crew to be rescued. Photo by Signal Magazine in August 1944

Until he returned, I waited alone in the woods with the three American crewmen. I wasn't scared because they acted very friendly and smiled at me a lot. One of them even held me on his lap. I still remember the jacket he wore. When he took it off to lay it on the ground, I noticed the American flag on the inside of the jacket. I remember running my finger over it. I recalled the time when my dad gave me a small American flag that looked like that when we first went to Snagov.

Another crewman wore a badge on his flight suit that looked to me like a funny little guy, the symbol of the 44th Bomb Group, I later learned. To me it looked like Mickey Mouse in the shape of a bomb.

The men seemed happy to be with me and gave me pliers to play with to keep me quiet, so nobody heard us. I did what they wanted. They rewarded me with a chocolate bar from the man resting on the trunk of a tree who gave me the signal to stay silent. I held it in my hand. When he saw that I didn't know what it was, he broke it open and gave me a piece to eat, the first taste of chocolate in my life. Later I felt this new taste was like a baptism for me to someday be an American kid. The last of the three gave me a small pencil which I kept for 65 years. I treasured it because it said Made in USA by the eraser. My mother brought this to me when she came to America to live in 1982.

Soon I slipped away to get my uncle and when he and I returned to the spot we heard nothing and saw nobody. My uncle held me by the hand and made a quiet little whistle. Turns out the wounded men decided to hide in a small ditch like a creek because they weren't sure of my uncle. It took awhile for them to realize that he intended to rescue them. They reappeared, my uncle helped them onto the cart and drove them to get medical aid. When we reached the infirmary, I told my uncle that he could go home. I would wait for my dad to come.

Two of the three airmen needed immediate help for injuries. I noticed one checked out a burn on his leg and said, "buba," which means a hurt. He smiled then pulled up his sleeve to show me his arm bleeding around his elbow. These two were sent to join some other injured airmen who needed medical attention. A German truck with a Romanian driver, my uncle later told me, picked them up and took them to downtown Bucharest to a burn hospital.

When the driver loaded them into the truck, I sneaked aboard to be with my two American "friends." When we arrived at the checkpoint, the officers found "a lost kid in the truck" which came from the Snagov infirmary. The driver sat me up front in the cab and continued driving to the Bucharest hospital, which included a special place for lost children so their parents could pick them up.

While the driver released the wounded men to the hospital, I walked with the driver to the back of the truck to say goodbye to my two friends. One took my hand and squeezed it tightly. The one with the injured arm took my head in his hands and kissed my forehead. I remember his lips were cold even on this very hot day. He told me to be a good boy. I remember him saying, boy, the word that I learned from the movies about cowboys.

Then the driver took me to the place for lost children. He told them where he picked me up. The hospital called the fire department at Snagov and gave them my name. I was already on the list as a lost child. My father and mother arrived to pick me up later that day.

Until that moment, I was fine. Now the time arrived for me to face my mother. I had a bad feeling that I faced big trouble. She was angry at my dad and my uncle for not keeping me with them. For too many hours she frantically looked for me. All I thought about was chocolate.

Later I found out my dad was detained and later released. He spent a few hours looking all over the place to find me. He didn't know anything I did with my uncle. The next day a Romanian soldier told him I slept at the gendarmerie and was fine.

When my mom and dad came to pick me up, they were told that one of the Americans said I was a tough kid. They said they felt safe and happy to have me with them to brighten their fearful hours. My father had this translated to him and later told me that the Americans gave me a big compliment.

These memories stayed with me throughout my life. The few hours I spent with these special Americans inspired me to think of nothing but how to get to the United States for the next twenty-four years and how I would manage to escape to get there.

I did finally escape from Communist Romania and found my way to America. I have since spent many years looking for surviving members of the crew. I wanted to thank them for my first American toy and in a roundabout way for making me a United States citizen in 1975.

Chapter Five:
Growing Up

I grew older, got into the higher grades, but America stayed with me every moment of my life. I attended a school closer to my home. My new teacher was an attractive lady. She acted, however, very mean when she expected the students to pay attention.

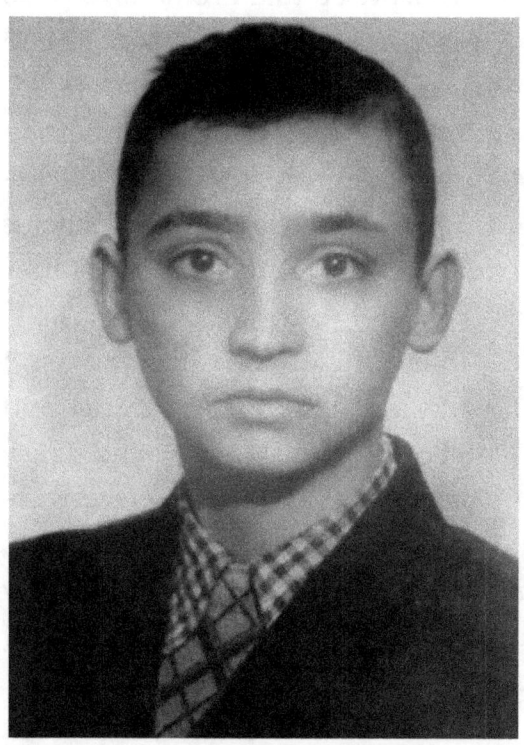

Cornell mandatory ID photo Age 14

In the class, many times instead of paying attention to the teacher, I kept busy drawing pictures of B24s or the American flag. I didn't look at her so right away she observed that I was otherwise involved.

She asked me to place my hands on the desktop and walked toward me and asked what I hid under the desk. I pulled out a piece of paper and showed her the B24 bomber dropping bombs.

In the corner I drew a small American flag.

She looked at it. "What is this?" she asked.

"I just remembered things," I said.

For that she punished me many times and made me stand in the corner of the room with my face turned to the wall, sometimes for more than twenty minutes. Many times, I had to kneel on broken walnut shells. In spite attempts by anyone to break me down for the next couple of years, I felt an inner determination and drew my pictures and the small flags whenever and wherever I could. The school called my mother in to show her what I did and gave drawings to her. My mother said it had to be related to the bombing raids during the war. When she told my dad, he was surprised that I remembered so clearly. He wasn't angry but instead put his arm around me and later took me to buy a pastry.

I managed to keep doing my drawings. I put them to good use whenever the teacher didn't show up. To keep the class from getting in trouble for too much noise, I told my classmates about the war. The kids kept quiet as they listened to my stories of the Ploesti bombing raids.

I also told them stories about scenes from the movies I remembered such as Zorro, Buffalo Bill, Tarzan, Laurel and Hardy, and the famous cowboys, John Wayne, and Gary Cooper, movies they would never see because now we were under Communist control.

The kids became so quiet listening to my stories that many times the school officials opened the door to see if the teacher had arrived.

Chapter Six:
My Military Experience

The next few years went by. When I was 19, I was ordered to appear at the draft board to take training as a soldier for an infantry unit.

While I and a group of other young men waited to be called in, some of them talked about the infantry being the hardest unit for basic training. I worried about what it would be like and how I would do.

After I was drafted, the board sent me off to infantry training. For the first couple of days, the training didn't seem too bad. After the first week, we received our full gear including rifles, backpacks, shovels, and some old boots that belonged to others before us. We all felt some impending doom. I slept on the top bunk, so I had a difficult time making the bed. I worried that I would be late and be punished.

In April it rained for two days. Our boots had no time to dry. We knew the worst part of basic training was about to take place.

Whenever the drill instructor, a typically rotten guy, entered our barracks to wake us up, he lit a wooden match. Then while he called us bastards and other worse names, he screamed at us that his finger was burning, and we had that little bit of time to get up, get dressed, get out and line up in front of the beds. Then he marched us outside and lined us up in the rain, sometimes in the middle of the night. He ordered us to throw ourselves face down in the mud because enemy planes were coming. Many still carried their boots and uniforms in their arms.

About a half hour later he ordered us to return to the barracks and to march and sing as we went. Soon, the entire platoon descended on the shower room to try to get the mud off our bodies, uniforms, and boots. We had all of ten or fifteen minutes to do that. During the clean up time, our drill instructor yelled, "Enemy planes knocked out the water supply!" He turned off all the water. We were forced to get back into our bunks wet and filthy with mud.

It was now perhaps one in the morning. The drill instructor did not allow us to light a fire to warm our barracks. We had to go to bed just as we were. We settled into our beds for about an hour, when suddenly the lights came on and we heard screams to get outside again in front of our barracks.

This time we were forced to run and pretend that we were under attack. It rained all night, and it seemed as if the barracks would get flooded. In the moment we went outside, we felt as if someone put a fire hose on us. He screamed at us to Run! Run! After we ran two times around the barracks, the drill instructor shouted at us that infantry fire had hit us. We had to go face down in a huge puddle of freezing cold water and mud. Then after we lined up, he ordered us to march to the barracks while singing again. Many of us thought we would never make it alive to the next day.

During this ordeal, one of my buddies, who came from the capital like me, a son of a doctor, refused to follow orders and had to do pushups outside in the rain after everybody went back inside. The next day he was called up in front of the unit for insubordination and for punishment was ordered to clean the latrines for an entire week.

When the rest of us returned to the showers we were surprised to find hot water. Everyone kept their mouths shut, sensing that someone made a mistake. We learned the truth later when the person responsible for the mistake was called up in front of the platoon and told that he must report to the commander and explain why he left the hot water on. Because he didn't obey orders, he was incarcerated for three days and made to sleep on plywood and eat only bread, water, and salt.

Later in the afternoon, ten of our guys were admitted to the infirmary with high fever and bronchitis. Six of us caught pneumonia. One went by emergency vehicle to the military hospital downtown with possible meningitis from high fever.

This was our typical routine for about two weeks. We heard a rumor that soon we would have to march twenty kilometers. We would have to wear our gas masks and run with them on. I was frightened when I heard this because I was susceptible to having bloody noses my entire life.

The next day we were forced to start marching. By the time we got about halfway, ten kilometers, the sun came out. We were still wearing our winter coats along with all our combat gear, including a blanket. We were not allowed to carry the rifle on our shoulder but had to hold it with one hand and had to keep it twenty inches above the ground, making our arm and hand numb. Sometimes the pain became unbearable and many of us would try to hold the rifle with both hands. We had to be careful not to be caught doing this because the punishment would be harsh.

About fifty yards ahead was a large crater made by a bomb. A drill instructor threw a smoke grenade into that crater and ordered us to put our masks on because he said poison gas was in the air. Then he told us to mount bayonets and attack the hill.

Our bodies were already overheated from ten kilometers of marching. We were soaked with sweat and with the masks on we had a difficult time breathing. When I put the mask on and tried to inhale, the mask immediately stuck to my face, and I didn't know what to do. The mask release valve didn't allow enough air in so you could breathe when you ran. After about twenty feet I fell into a ditch, unable to see because my goggles were full of blood. Seconds later, I passed out. I was told that my drill sergeant swore at me to get up and not to dare remove the mask because I would be court martialed. One of my buddies noticed my distress and the position in which I fell. He said to the sergeant, "Sir, I think he's dead!" Not believing him, the sergeant proceeded to kick me in the behind. When he saw no reaction, he asked one of the men to remove the mask from my face. In the moment they pulled the mask from my face the sergeant noticed that the blood had coagulated. His face turned white. He realized he was in deep trouble because there was no help around and he had no way to communicate with the base in case anybody got severely hurt. Two of the soldiers had to run to a nearby highway to stop a car to get back to the base to summon help. In the meantime, a few guys washed my face with water from their own canteens so I could remove the dried blood from my nose and my mouth to allow me to breathe air.

About 45 minutes later an ambulance picked me up and took me to the military hospital where I was kept for four weeks. From there I was sent home and six months later I was called back for duty

Chapter Seven:
A Lucky Break

One day I received a letter from the recruiting center that shocked me. I thought that after the accident they considered me disabled. After carefully reading the letter, I saw they wanted me to appear before the medical board for reevaluation.

By the end of the month, I sat on a train on my way to the border between Romania and Bulgaria to a city called Mangalia.

This time they sent me to the Navy. For two days I worked on a small frigate doing a lot of cleaning. The frigate was anchored in the harbor for about two months. Most of the sailors on board were going home after their third year. In 1959, the Romanian Navy dropped the requirement of service from three years to two years.

One afternoon, at about four o'clock, another sailor told me to mop up the stern area of the ship and call him when I finished for an inspection. While I mopped, one of the older three-year sailors walked into the area where I cleaned and intentionally kicked over the bucket filled with soap. The soap spilled on his pants. He screamed that I ruined his pants and should lick the soap off or he would send me back to my ---- Mother. He used a foul word. After my recent experience in the infantry in basic training, which almost killed me, it didn't take too long to get my adrenaline up. I said to him, leave my mother out of it you son-of-a-bitch! I dropped the mop and swung a punch and hit him as hard as I could in his lower right jaw. He slipped on the soapy water and hit the chain at the edge of the deck and fell right into the water. Some other sailors who witnessed the incident immediately restrained me. They called the shore patrol and I soon found myself under arrest.

They talked about court-martialing me but later found out that for me to be court-martialed I had to already be sworn in. The next day they released me because I wasn't part of the military. The Commanding Officer told me he'd transferred me to another unit of the engineers which specialized in building bridges and other construction required during combat. Since it was peacetime, most of the units constructed homes and new barracks on the bases. Until they found the right place for me, they sent me to the kitchen to peel potatoes.

When I was first drafted, my military file showed I had a driver's license from the capital and that I worked with government officials as a driver there. To possess a driver's license from the capital, I was required to take a special two-year training course as a Certified Mechanic, which placed me in a higher qualification bracket as a driver. It didn't take them very long to find out that this recruit had a lot of valuable experience.

One day while I sat on a bucket outside the kitchen peeling potatoes, a Russian made jeep, a Gaz 67, drove up and stopped by the curb. I was surprised to see this senior officer staring at me.

When I looked away, he asked, "Are you Iliescu?"

I stood up. "Yes, Sir."

"Why are you here?"

"I don't know."

He said, "What do you mean, you don't know. You didn't punch anybody in the face?"

"Yes, sir, I did, but he called my mother a bitch."

"How did you do it? Can you show me?"

I swung my fist in the air to show him.

He said, "No, come here and hit me."

"No, I can't do that, sir."

He raised his palm in the air. "Go ahead. Let me see how hard you hit him."

When I did it, he said, "You're pretty good, you son-of-a gun! Do you have a driver's license?"

"Yes, Sir."

"May I see it?" he asked.

After I showed it to him, he asked, "You see this guy?" He pointed to his driver. "He was supposed to go home a month ago and I need to find a driver before he can leave. Do you want to be my driver?"

My heart was in my throat. I don't know how I answered but I almost choked myself with my answer of yes.

Within an hour his driver, a corporal, returned to pick me up and to take me to the uniform depository for me to get fitted out with brand new totally different type of overalls and a Class A uniform.

Then the driver took me downtown to the headquarters to show me the room which I would share with a couple of guards, a telephone operator, and a maintenance man. In the space of a couple of hours my life changed completely from downheartedly peeling potatoes to nervously waiting outside of the commanding officer's door to report for duty.

Minutes later, I knocked on the door and when the door opened, I saw the commander at his desk meeting with two other officers. I glanced around the huge empty room with a window behind his desk, a small desk for his secretary on the right and a bookcase on the left.

I walked up to his desk, stood before him, saluted, and said, "Sir, I am Private Iliescu reporting for duty."

He stood up, reached his hand forward and shook my hand. The other officers had to stand because he did.

He said, "You already look a lot better. I hope you will take good care of me and my car."

"You will never regret it because I will do my best."

He turned to the other officers. "This is my new driver who comes from my hometown of Bucharest."

Cornell in Summer 1958 as driver for Romanian army base commander

During the two years I worked for Lieutenant Colonel Michael Niculescu, Engineer, our relationship became like two good buddies. He never made me feel inferior to him. We talked and sang together. We ate together and stayed in the same hotel. He made me feel like his brother. Whenever he went to a conference in the capital, he gave me permission to go on leave to visit my family. I could even wear civilian clothes. A few times we met on the train and ended up sitting in the same cabin.

One time my commander told me that I was born in the wrong country. Without saying it to each other, we knew that the Communists' ideas were not part of our lives. He recognized how my behavior was different from the rest of the soldiers. We shared the same thoughts about the future.

He was right. I waited to meet the right people at the right time. When I completed my two years of service and prepared to go home, he faced a problem: finding a driver. He decided to let me go home for two weeks and then hired me back as a civilian driver. This commander and I stayed good friends for a long time and shared many common ideas.

In the summer of 1960, we both came home driving in a big truck. He rode with me in the back of the truck for the entire 300-kilometer trip, which took about five to six hours to go from the base to the Bucharest headquarters. During the trip, he sang all the arias he knew at the top of his voice. By the time we got home he could hardly speak. Our friendship continued until 1968 when I escaped from Romania.

Chapter Eight: Coming Home

When I returned home, I spent time with my family. The local authorities were rebuilding the capital city of Bucharest. The streets were filled with demolition and reconstruction.

My father worked for a construction company. My brother got involved in the construction as a Lieutenant with the Military Corps of Engineers since the government required them to help rebuild the city.

I spent time with my friends and looked for a place to work. A very good friend told me about the company where his wife worked, which happened to be near to my house. The company purchased a new truck and needed a driver. With my driving experience I got hired right away. I drove the truck around the capital, picked up materials and distributed them elsewhere.

At this time the situation with the government made it difficult to live. They considered every person to be an enemy of the state. They stripped the people of every right. The government could search your home any time they chose. They confiscated everything, including your home, your car, your bicycle, and especially your radio.

No such thing as privacy existed. They could even read your mail. We lived each day not knowing if we would be alive tomorrow. No one was really your friend. If you had a job, someone would want that job. He could easily say something bad about you and you'd be arrested and never be free again.

They took our home and threw us into a room. Four people in the room. No bathroom and only one toilet for five families.

Chapter Nine:
Music in my Life

During the forties my father bought a little plot of land which the Communists never found out about. He wanted to someday build a small house away from the city. It never materialized although my brother and I did manage to get the foundation dug and some brick walls put up. In the sixties my parents decided they would never have the money to finish the house, so they decided to sell it. They sold it to some people out in the country and gave my brother and me some of what they realized from the sale. With the money I bought a small portable reel-to-reel recorder made in Czechoslovakia by Tesla.

Immediately after that I started to spend nights recording music from wherever I could find it. I collected the songs of Frank Sinatra, Dean Martin, Ray Charles, and Elvis Presley in my room. Most of the music I liked came from the United States. Many times, I took my music player to work, where we enjoyed dancing after work hours.

Most of the young people were amazed at my music and my way of dancing. From the time when I was a little boy, I enjoyed watching dancing whenever and wherever I saw it. My parents and their friends danced. I enjoyed the sound of the big bands on the radio.

I gathered more friends who enjoyed the music they'd never heard before. Some were students of music and played different instruments. From then on, their behavior and style of music changed completely. We began to hold dance parties in different friends' homes.

The government came to realize that the youth were very hard to control because they were feeling the influence of the West. Ideas from England, Italy, France, and Germany were impossible to avoid and were embraced by the young. Slowly the shackles came off.

Chapter Ten:
I get Married

At my job, I made a lot of friends who appreciated my enthusiasm. During some of the company gatherings, leaders of the company talked about having Saturday night dances and inviting the people in the company to come and have a good time.

Soon, a lot of volunteers gathered to decorate the hall for the occasion. We asked the company to provide some amplification so we could have a good sound system. When our first Saturday arrived, all the excited ladies tried to find their best dresses to wear and hoped for new dance partners. Young men and women showed up from other company locations.

The sound of the music was new to them and each danced in his own way. Everyone did his best to make the most of the rhythms. Not many were familiar with rock and roll, swing, or ballroom dancing but those of us who met and danced together privately since the fifties shared what we knew. We took turns dancing with many different partners so everyone would have a fun time.

Some people pointed out a pretty girl with black hair and dark eyes sitting on the sidelines. They told me that she knew how to dance well.

At first, she was shy and said, "I don't dance."

I said, "Everyone came to learn. If you try to follow along, you'll do fine."

From the moment we started dancing I knew she had rhythm and the ability to do well. After that she became an excellent dance partner. We danced a lot at private parties, spent a lot of time together, and soon made plans to get married.

We had a small wedding at home because her father was a factory director. To be a factory director, he had to be a member of the Communist Party. We could not, therefore, risk a church wedding. We called the priest to her home for the ceremony. Friends and family joined us. The next day we traveled to the mountains for our honeymoon

Chapter Eleven:
A Better Position

My wife, Melania, stayed at the job where we met but I wanted a better job. When changing jobs, I wanted to improve my position, so I'd be involved with more influential people in the government without being a member of the Communist Party.

From a group of friends, I found out about an important government division that needed an experienced driver with a high school education.

This division controlled all printed material from the news, books, magazines, and newspapers. The name of it was Directia Generala a Presei si Tipariturilor. This office controlled so much that if anybody wanted to write a song or present a play, the lyrics or script needed approval of the controller first to make sure it included no negative words against the government.

The controllers closely watched every theatre or studio and investigated every piece of writing and, if necessary, stopped and arrested everyone involved.

Despite all these restrictions, I later convinced these powerful men to accept and listen to my band group, Sincron, the first group after WWII to perform in public on electric guitars and to imitate the American style of rock and roll music.

Within a year the censors allowed them to appear on a television show and even play Wooly Bully without using any of the English words. They even traveled to Communist bloc countries including Russia, where they had great success.

The driving job sounded interesting to me, so I got more information about it and heard that I needed to be interviewed by a big boss there. After filling out my application and getting interviewed at the personnel office for about two hours, they said I had to meet the high official and he would decide whether I qualified for the job. A few people I knew there were surprised to hear that I had to meet "the big boss" just to get a driver position They didn't ever remember this happening before. They advised me to be very careful with my answers when I spoke to him because during the late thirties that man had been in the same jail as Nicolai Ceaucescu, the current president of Romania.

My new boss was a cellmate of Nicolai Ceausescu. They were arrested for stealing bread from the bakery. The truth was that they were arrested for distributing Communist flyers. In their everyday lives they played at being Communists. They acted as if they were the most powerful people on earth and made their own rules and yet when they entertained themselves, they listened to music and entertainment from the West that they allowed no one else to experience.

I wasn't afraid of the interview but was mostly curious about why he wanted to meet me. I knew I had a good clear driving record and a good relationship with anyone I drove in the past.

The next day, the head of the personnel office called me in. "The interview will begin in about ten minutes," he said. I was dressed up in a suit, tie, and white shirt, not typical for a driver at the time. It seemed to open doors for me. I took an elevator to the fifth floor and then went through some huge doors. In front of me two ladies sat at a desk.

One asked, "Are you Iliescu?"

I said, "Yes."

The other said, "Sit down and wait."

A few minutes later a white phone sitting between a black and a red one, rang. The woman spoke into the phone, "Tovaras (Comrade) Iliescu is here."

When I entered the room, I saw a short grey-haired man sitting at a huge desk with a stony expression on his face. He had big eyes and bushy eyebrows. For a few minutes he continued reading a newspaper. Then he took his glasses off, lifted his head up and looked directly into my eyes. I was standing about ten feet away. His first words were, "Oh, you do look different! Why do you want to work here?"

I said, "I enjoy driving new cars and I like to be around important people."

He said, "I can appreciate that, but in order for that to happen you should be a member of the Communist Party."

"Besides being a driver," I said, "I am a promoter and work with the sound equipment for bands. I'm very busy with that."

He said, "Oh yeah, what do you promote?"

"A band called Sincron. We have four good guitar players and a piano player, and they're now appearing at the theatre, The Teatru De Estrada, pe Calea Victoriei."

He seemed impressed. "I'm surprised I don't know about them."

"I'd be happy for you to come and listen sometime."

He said, "Yes, I will arrange to listen to them in my own clubhouse."

He made a few notes then looked up. "Can you start working anytime?"

I said, "Yes, Sir!"

"I like your attitude," he said. "Return to the personnel office for further instructions."

When I got there, the manager told me I would start the next day at 7 a.m. He gave me the keys. Then he called a driver to bring the car around. He explained all the details about where to get gas, where to go for maintenance, and where to park the car at night. The car assigned to me was one of the largest Russian cars, a Volga sedan, a copy of the German Opel Capitan. I was thrilled with it because I had never driven one before.

When I arrived at work on my first day, they gave me a schedule of the times they needed me. I would drive him to a performance at the opera that first night. I would wait until the show ended and then bring him home.

When I drove him from home to the opera, he sat in the back seat and never said a word. When he entered the car, he said, "You know where we are going."

I said, "Yes."

The pass on the window meant that we didn't get stopped and went straight through the police barriers. My license plate had special letters on it which made them aware that this was a VIP car.

That night I felt more important than the person I was driving. I felt as if I held the world in my hands. I thought to myself, if I got here, I could get anywhere.

While I waited in front of the theater, I met a few other drivers who also drove for important government people. I noticed that I was the youngest one and the only one in a suit.

When the opera concluded, all the drivers lined up their cars. When my turn came, I saw my boss waiting on the curb talking to someone. I jumped out of the car and opened the door. He continued his conversation and when the other person said, "Oh, is this your new driver?" he bid him goodbye and got into the car.

When I started to drive home, he said, "I really enjoyed the program."

I asked, "Which opera did you see?"

He said, "The Arias from Verdi."

"I saw that one and liked it, too."

"Oh, you like opera," he said.

I answered, "I like all music."

"How old are you?"

"27."

"Where did you learn to drive," he asked.

I said, "My dad taught me when I was a boy of 14 and he drove large construction trucks."

When we arrived at the place where I would drop him off, he said, "It was nice of you to open the door for me but please don't do that again. I can open my own doors."

In thinking about this later I felt that he liked the idea, but it didn't fit with his ideology. By having this job, I learned more about the Communist System of Government and what it really stood for, the differences between what they told the people and what the reality was.

Chapter Twelve: Music

In the beginning of the sixties the Beatles became famous around the world. The Romanians weren't allowed to bring them into the country, nor could they afford that. We were, however, able to get copies of their music through underground channels.

Then, almost overnight, their music was all we played or heard. We experienced Beatlemania in Romania, too. The other countries of the Eastern Communist Bloc welcomed the British music invasion, but Romania placed a very serious restriction on any Western information of any kind.

One night I went to visit a family friend I thought of as an uncle, Gheorge Farcasi. His stage name was Jimmy Sinclair. He went to America with his parents as a child and moved to New York where he worked as a dancer at a Broadway theatre in the early 30's. He became an accomplished American choreographer, well known at the time. After the war, when he was ready for retirement, he decided to use what money he'd saved to buy property in Romania and live there.

After World War II, Romania became a Communist country. The Communists methodically confiscated the entire country, homes, businesses, properties. They took his property and gave him and his wife a tiny room in which to live, leaving him in a state of shock. At age 60 his money was gone, and his musical career was behind him. Now he used his other talent as a men's tailor to survive. He later became the top tailor in the capital city of Bucharest.

He also worked in the Variety Theatre on wardrobes and helped with choreography. While I talked to him during one of his rehearsals, a young man passed by and greeted him with a "Hi Jimmy."

I asked, "Who was that?"

"His name is Emil Kost. He organized a small band called Sincron. They'll play a few minutes during the evening performance."

I met Emil later in the hallway, introduced myself and told him about my interest in music. We set up a time to talk later. After I watched the band perform, I got excited and visualized being a part of what they were doing. I saw this band could be big. Emil came over to my house and we listened to all the music I had recorded in the last few years. We made plans to work together, which included rehearsing in my house. My parents loved it. We all became very close friends.

Through that chance meeting we worked together on the music and established a group that became a "Top Ten" band for eight years.

Our band, Sincron, became well known and overnight found ourselves live on National TV. When this happened, when Sincron had its own television show, we thought we were exempt from the typical scrutiny others experienced at that time. We thought we were on the way to freedom of expression since the Government accepted the English language and music.

We were very wrong! One night we were invited to play for a live television program. The show was like *Romania's Got*

Talent and was called *The Star without a Name.* After a few performances, the public wanted Sincron to play a song which they were known for and had success with.

The audience started to whistle and shout, *Wooly Bully!* But something terrible happened earlier, backstage, minutes before the show started. Our drummer brought a small bottle of Cognac and passed it around to the band members thinking it would diminish their stage fright and that they would play better.

When the curtain opened, the band broke through some huge paper replicas of playing cards to get to the stage. The audience went out of control and for more than ten minutes the show couldn't start because of the bedlam and the throwing of shoes, hats, and clothing up in the air in their enthusiasm for what they would be hearing. Finally, the band started to play, and the enthusiasm heightened. The audience carried on, shouting for us to play *Wooly Bully!*

After a few songs the band finally began to play *Wooly Bully*. The audience went out of control. One of the camera men took his headphones off and threw his hat on the stage. Security couldn't put a stop to the situation because they, too, got carried away with the enthusiasm of the audience over what was happening on the stage. The piano player, also the main singer, swung the microphone in the air and imitated the gyrations of Elvis Presley. The bass player knelt and the drummer stood up and beat the drums like a madman. One of the guitar players turned the amplifier up higher so he could hear himself.

After only about a minute, the main control suddenly turned the sound off. The place didn't get quieter.

Some big government officials passed the word to silence everything until the show ended. But the show continued through the evening with no sound and no television broadcasting. The audience knew nothing of the blocking of the sound on the TV.

The next day the main newspaper in town reported about the hooligans on stage in a show the night before. The reporter used the most disgraceful words. It sounded as if we weren't even human.

Of course, our punishment was harsh. They suspended us for one entire year. We couldn't to play or sing anywhere in public, banned us from singing any songs with English words, and forbade American music.

We could play music without words. They told us to completely change our repertoire. We had to play Romanian folk music in our own way. Our music director and band leader came up with the idea to write folk music with a country rock beat. After eight months of hard work and many rehearsals we had enough songs to record an album.

That was our salvation and the beginning of our recovery. We were permitted to make the album and now, once again, we were great in the eyes of those who had put us in the gutter. The public accepted us with open arms. After two appearances in public, we went back into first place on the charts.

A month later the government invited us to appear at a studio to begin making a movie. It took about six months and was called *Eight Minutes of Dreams.* The movie hit the theaters soon after and it experienced great success. We started traveling around our country and the neighboring Socialist countries again. In 1968, when I made my escape from Romania, our band, Sincron, faced huge competition from other young bands. Fifteen years later, when I returned to Romania, I learned that most of the band members had emigrated to other countries such as USA and Greece. The band leader, Cornell Fugaru was the only one who became a Communist sympathizer. He later became an obese heavy drinker and passed away in 2011 at the age of 68.

Chapter Thirteen:
The Relationship

Melania and I spent several years together working on our relationship. Our biggest challenge was that she couldn't have children. I feared this because we had already spent a lot of time together and she never conceived.

Because to me having a family was very important, I felt uncertain about getting married. My parents, however, especially my mother, felt that being in a relationship for more than a year obligated me to marry her. It wasn't that she liked her so much but that the honor of our families was at stake.

This infertility issue ultimately led to our breakup. Her doctor referred her to a clinic, a beautiful spa called Sovata in the mountains of Transylvania, which had been around since Roman times. Its mineral springs had curative powers.

While she was there, she met a worker, a bookkeeper, and they started a relationship. To impress her, he spent the government's money for a month of partying and fun times. This did not compare to our meager existence.

When she returned home, she encouraged him to move to Bucharest to be close to her. He came for a vacation and after about a month the authorities from the clinic caught up with him. They found a large amount of money missing from the government account. He was subsequently arrested and sentenced to two years in prison.

She tried to help him by borrowing money from her grandparents. The grandparents got frightened because of the large amount she asked for. They immediately called a family gathering. They talked to her parents and when she came home from work the grandparents were sitting on the sofa at her parents' house.

She was confident as she approached the house. In her mind she didn't feel she had done anything wrong. In the moment she saw her grandparents she realized the whole family knew everything. She felt tearful and ashamed. She had no other choice but to tell the truth.

To her father, she caused a great embarrassment. Because she disgraced the family, they gave her two choices. One, back to her husband. Second, move out on her own. She felt that to go back to me was out of the question because she didn't know if I would accept her. It would also be very humiliating in front of her coworkers, her friends, and my family. She asked them to give her some time to move out on her own.

It wasn't easy to find a place to live. She finally settled for a poor house with no heat or running water and a toilet in the back yard.

At that time, I no longer worked for the same company. A friend of hers later contacted me and told me that she needed some of her bedding. She was in bad shape and needed help and compassion because her parents disowned her. We were apart for about two years at the time. I went to her job site and waited for her. I picked her up in my company car and took her to a place where we could talk. She had lost a lot of weight. Her clothing was shabby.

She walked with her head down and avoided eye contact with me. I knew of a place where we could eat. She described

The Relationship

her situation and refused to invite me to her room because it was small and depressing with no table or chairs. She had a little Godin, a small round cast iron stove, but no firewood. I felt bad for her.

After we finished eating, I went home to pick up the bedding and went to a friend who had some firewood and borrowed a few logs for her. She suggested that I wait a few days until she could fix up the room with a table someone had promised her. I insisted that I bring the wood and bedding right away because the nights were freezing cold. A few days later I brought her some food which she heated up on the little stove. We ate this while sitting on the edge of the bed, talking about how to get her out of the predicament she was in.

She fixed some Turkish coffee and came close to me to tell me something. She put the coffee on the floor and squatted in front of me. Talking in a very small voice she asked if I could ever forgive her. I did not find it easy to find the words to say how I felt. I recalled so well the heartbreaking moment after she returned from treatment and announced to me that she had a new man in her life. She no longer wanted to be with me. It broke my heart. I experienced great pain and torment after ten years of marriage.

Now, even though my heart went out to her, I felt compassion rather than revenge. I was very sorry for her but knew that she would have to live with what she did for the rest of her life. I fought with myself to keep in mind how much I had gone through. I couldn't throw her to the wolves, so we continued talking about getting her out of the mess she was in.

Chapter Fourteen: My Livelihood

I had great experience from my job in the military and the relationships that I built with my other bosses after the military. When I returned home from the military service, I found a job through friends driving a small van carrying supplies around the city. After a few years working there, I became tired of the menial tasks of a company truck driver. I wanted a better job than delivering chemical supplies, loading, and unloading, in the Bucharest surrounding area. Instead of wearing dirty work clothes I wanted to wear a nice suit, shirt, and tie.

That's when I heard about the driving job for a government official, took the interview, and changed my lifestyle. I wasn't always driving for one person. I never knew what my assignment would be or where I would be going. This lasted a couple years but then I was assigned to the night shift because I was the youngest driver in the group. I was newly married but with no children. That put me in a place where I started to look for a day job.

My final job in Romania came at a time in my life when I was also looking for more freedom. I wanted to find a job with better pay and hoped to find one where I could travel in the West. One thing that came naturally to me was to be enthusiastic. I always admired and appreciated people and I guess it showed when I met others.

During the sixties in Romania, everything in the country was owned by the government. You couldn't look for a job. You had to be referred and transferred within the system.

I heard about a job in the Ministry of Art. and asked to be transferred there as a driver. This appealed to me because of the caliber of people I'd be working with. The job involved driving the car with my boss to and from different foreign embassies. Every day I'd listen to different languages and be around very highly educated people.

After I got the job, I found myself included as part of the group, not as a driver but as an art official. The director, Mircea Deac, seemed to like the way I presented myself and treated me well. Many times, he took time out to talk about the artworks we were involved with. My director was very highly educated. He was a graduate of the Academy of Art in Paris. He was fluent in French, Romanian, and English. I always enjoyed his company and his calm demeanor. He had a wonderful manner, soft spoken and elegant. He knew all about my life and about the sadness of the breakup with my wife. He gave me good advice.

He also suspected and knew about my later relationship with his secretary during my separation from my wife. One day, I told him that my wife needed my help because she was in bad shape living in an uninhabitable place. I wanted to make up with her and have a nice place for her but not with my parents since they were unforgiving. He said that he might be able to help me. His father-in-law was a reputable doctor in Romania. After the war he was allowed to keep some of his property. He told me about a room that I could rent. Before long Melania and I were looking for furniture. We didn't need too much because the place was small but cozy. It was a big improvement. Our relationship was going smoothly but I always had a negative feeling about what had happened between us.

After the two-year breakup, this was the first time that I lived away from my family and once again with my wife. It was good for us to be alone together and away from the pressures of both families. Our relationship got better every day.

For my boss, the director, it was much more convenient now that I lived in the same building as he did. We could go to work together. I was within easy reach whenever he needed me.

But in the back of my mind something never changed and that something was the idea of freedom off on the distant horizon. This involved a plot that I put together over four years and about which no one knew. Any person in the family that knew could cause a disaster, not intentionally, but through love could cause a life in prison for me.

During the last four years, very devoted friends quietly worked on our big escape. Every day we got closer and closer. Each of us became more quiet and more emotional than ever.

We were concerned and afraid a leak could happen up to the last second and we could be picked up as suspects just because of our quiet behavior. I couldn't tell anyone, not my wife, my parents, my friends. I could trust no one. When the moment finally came, we were filled with fear and anticipation. There was no turning back. We were on the way to freedom.

Chapter Fifteen:
Sincron and My Escape

My life was very much involved with the band, which later became my lifesaver.

One day during a rehearsal, one of my friends who enjoyed his association with Sincron, a well-educated man who spoke English, French, and Italian, asked me to join him for coffee.

Without talking too much, we knew we shared the same dream: America. Emil, a tall young man with a determined attitude., knew survivor skills from his college years when he worked as an outdoor guide.

He loved outdoor adventures and told me he knew well the country in and around the Carpathian Mountains. After several meetings, I brought my friend Victor into the group. He was a good organizer, so we gave him the job of planning an escape for us from our homeland. With the three of us our hopes grew stronger. Victor talked for three years about an escape, but we were just a couple of kids with no serious plan.

Now, in only two months we had three people on board. The stakes were so high we dared not talk to anyone, even each other, about our plans.

One day I visited an old friend, Fane (Stefan), an orphan since WWII. He was very poor and quit school at the age of 7 to work and support himself. He worked for a company washing cars and now could service them, too.

When I met him, he was busy and asked me to hang around and wait for him. Soon he finished and invited me to lunch since he had gotten a good tip and could afford to be generous. He wanted to treat me since I usually invited him. I was surprised but wondered why he did that. When we got to the Buffet Express, he asked me what I wanted to eat but there wasn't much of a choice. I think we ate mashed potatoes, sausage, a roll, and rice pudding. At that time, you could also find Pepsi. While we waited for the food, I was struck when he asked some very direct questions. At first, I didn't know how to answer but he repeated what he asked.

Then he drew close to me and whispered, "Cornell, I have known for a long time that you want to run away. Let's go together! I know a way, but it is only a 50-50 chance of survival." He paused and then said, "I cannot live like an animal anymore."

I asked, "How do you know how to escape?"

He said, "I learned from correspondence with other friends."

He mentioned a few names. Some sounded familiar. At first, I was wary. I felt he must have been so desperate that he became an undercover agent for the Securitate. I was easy prey, I figured, and if he chose to turn me in, one of his best friends, they would believe him without question. It would be very good for his career.

We exchanged a few more words. He insisted he knew the best way to escape. He pleaded with me to go with him. I now waited for the unexpected to happen.

Two or three days went by. I didn't think much about my talk with Fane.

Then he showed up at my work. "I want to talk with you."

We sat in a park across the street where he pulled out a piece of paper with the plan for the escape.

He startled me so much I told him to put it away quickly. We talked a bit more and then split up. After that I decided that I should explain what happened with Fane to my other two friends. After giving the incident some thought, we three talked then decided to go ahead and include him. He showed determination, strength, and a willingness to risk his life.

Our group was now ready to proceed. Each one of us took on a specific assignment but we all knew the importance of choosing a leader.

Our team included Emil, our well-educated leader who specialized in sports medicine; a handyman, Victor; an auto serviceman, Fane; and impresario/chauffeur, Cornell. This band of brothers determined to face whatever would happen and looked forward to a free world.

During the next few months, we put ourselves through intense self-imposed training. Every minute counted. We spent time on survival training in the mountains. After eight months of training under rough conditions, our leader heard from different sources that the Organizatia Nationala de Tourism was taking applications for people of any age to tour the West. If they had the money to deposit, 2500 lei, they could go.

It seemed like an opportune event for us to use for our purposes. We got funds together after several months from friends and helpful family members.

One by one, we went to the travel office and asked for the applications, which were nothing but questionnaires. Then the nightmares started. Everyday we were deluged with requests to drop off more documents with proof of income, employment, etc. The most serious request came from the highest-ranking government official at each of our jobs. From the moment that we applied and completed our requests to travel in the Western countries, notifications were made to various official organizations. One was to the Sectorist of my neighborhood, part of the police station near my home. This individual knew exactly who I was, who my friends were, what visitors came to my house, how often they came, and many other incidental yet personal activities that related to me. Everyone in the country had a Sectorist. Each of these local officials reported on the behavior and activity of every citizen. My job was also notified as soon as the papers for the trip were processed. This same thing also happened to each one of my friends.

The Sectorist for me happened to be the husband of one of my cousins. They were separated at the time, and he kept a very sharp eye on me. He disliked me for many reasons such as the music I favored, the way I danced, my choice of friends, and lastly because I never became a member of the Communist Party. For him it seemed ironic that I worked for a very important institution which allowed me access to some important government people. I learned that he sent a negative report about me to the officials.

A few weeks later my partners received approval to travel and were ready to go. Everyone except me. Discouraged and depressed, I didn't know what to do. At this time in my life, having been separated again for a few years from my wife, I got in touch with an old friend of mine. She ran the Personnel Office at my work, especially concerning related Communist Activities. She knew me well, felt close to me, and proceeded to send a favorable report about her coworker to a high-level member of the Communist Party.

A week before the tourist company planned to complete its list and advise the people to pay the balance, I was still waiting and hoping for a miracle. We all felt a lot of tension as to whether to proceed with the plans or wait for another time.

Friday morning at about 10 o'clock I received a call from the passport office that they approved me to go on the tour. Without much fuss, I let my friends know that I'd be with them because I received the okay. We were all relieved but still fearful about the outcome of our plans.

I prepared a small suitcase with the essentials. To celebrate our approval of the trip and review our plans we went to a place in the mountains, a ski resort, Sura Dacilor, a hotel-restaurant where mostly foreign tourists visited. When we traveled, we were very careful to make sure that no police or secret agents followed us. We returned to our homes the next day to prepare ourselves to face the unthinkable.

Next came the most difficult moment in our lives that one never hopes to experience. For me it was saying goodbye to my mother, my father, and my brother whom I knew I might never see again. They only understood that I was going away for a few days with my friends. My wife returned to me by this time, and she acted a little suspicious and showed strange behavior. We didn't have enough time to talk about what she suspected was going on.

The moment of highest tension occurred when we got a taxi to get to the place where the bus waited for us. When we arrived, we stood in line and handed in our luggage. One by one they loaded us into the bus. We knew that besides the two drivers two more informants were on the bus. One of the drivers called out the name of each person. We were not allowed to keep our passports. They filled his hands.

About 45 people boarded the bus. Most were over 60. We were the only younger ones except for two ladies in their 40's.

When I looked into their eyes, they all seemed equally scared as we waited for the bus to start. When we drove along the highway, the usual behavior was to laugh or sing.

Soon I made a few jokes with the two ladies and got people singing. Others joined in and began to enjoy themselves, including the two drivers who up until now had never smiled.

We spent the first night on the Romanian border eating with the rest of the group and having fun. It felt good to relax a little and it appeared most natural that we would do that.

The next day, after about an hour of driving, we crossed the Yugoslavian border. Each of us found a female friend to sit with, which fit in with our portrayal of a holiday spirit. I sat with a very friendly lady and found a lot to talk to her about.

When the bus stopped at a rest area, we continued our private talk. She gave me some advice. She said she knew I was not returning from this trip. She sensed that but I was not sure how. More important, she wanted me to know that one of the passengers in the front of the bus overheard a conversation between the two drivers. They said that they should call and report the suspicious behavior of the four young guys before crossing the Hungarian border. I guess we looked too happy to them. They wondered why. It was possible that we could be arrested and sent back to Romania. Her last words to me were, "Go and don't look back." She said there was nothing for us in Romania and this might be our one chance to live a different life.

When we approached the Hungarian border, we weren't sure how far we had to go. We knew that it was time for us to make a big decision. Behind our bus a car had followed us for a long time. We acted as though we didn't notice it, but we were all scared. At almost lunch time, we approached a little town. The bus stopped at a nice hotel where we used the restroom for the last time. We knew that now was the hour for us to make our move.

We went around the hotel so we would not be seen and then started to walk. Without warning, Emil suddenly jumped in front of a passing taxi and hissed at us to get in. We hurriedly guided the driver on a circuitous route through the town and directed him to take us to the train station.

There we found out exactly where we were and how far we were from Italy. We estimated that the money we had left would help us to travel approximately 175 kilometers by train. We also figured that we had perhaps 250 kilometers to reach our destination.

We couldn't use all the money we had because we had to save some for desperate emergencies. Emil told us that now we could relax because the danger was behind us. But now we had to decide when and how to get started. We bought the tickets and boarded the train. At this point we still looked very presentable and blended in well with the rest of the people.

After traveling 175 kilometers we left the train to spend the night in the station. We were still in Yugoslavia. It was the beginning of the summer with warm days and cool evenings. We managed fine. In the morning, we found something to eat and then began the challenging part of our venture.

First, we had to know the direction we needed to go. Some of us wanted to try hitching a ride but Emil was not comfortable with that. Finally, he came up with the idea to signal only the trucks and cars with foreign license plates. We found ourselves in the middle of this small town trying to locate the direction to the highway we needed. On every corner we saw someone who looked like they were watching us. For our own safety we crossed streets and got into marketplaces where we could disappear into the crowds. Very near to us we saw a coffee shop.

While waiting for our order, I heard a group of people speaking Italian. I asked Emil if it might be okay to ask these people directions. Emil thought it all right but admonished me to be very careful when they asked me questions in return. We knew that the Romanian government offered big rewards for the return of any of its Romanian citizens. My heart was in my throat when I started the conversation, but I did my best to cover my fear. I said that I recognized their Italian language and I wanted to know if they knew of any bus that was going to Italy.

His response was, "Ciao, mio nome e' Franco!"

I answered, "Mio nome Corneliu."

He was not from that area but told me that he could take us for about 25 kilometers going toward his home. We were happy for the offer from this nice, friendly man. He even gave us an address when we later reached Italy to go to his house.

We reached the point where we needed to hitch rides to get where we needed to go. Finally, a truck stopped and asked us where we were going. We told him that we were going in the same direction he was headed, and asked if he would take us as far as he could. He had a stop coming up in about 28 kilometers and could take us that far.

He stopped in a small town at 1 a.m. We saw no place to hide so we headed towards the woods. Most of the following nights we slept near trees and in trenches by highways so we would not be noticed nor lose the direction we were going.

During the colder nights we stole clothing we found in backyards to cover ourselves.

For our main food, we ate wild fruits we found along the way. I was the skinniest of them all and they worried about me. They were concerned if I would be able to make it. They knew my desire and determination and hoped I wouldn't get too physically weak to survive the ordeal. On this our third night, we all felt the urgent need for real food.

One night we got the impression that three men were following us. We noticed that they had bats and knives, so in a desperate moment we hid in the tunnel of the city sewer. They saw the direction we went and started to follow us, but we managed to disappear. Now our survival training came to our minds, but we had no idea what would happen.

To get out of the tunnel we walked all the way to the main manhole, where we saw a little light coming through. Sometimes we were up to our necks in the sewage and water and the smell made us gag and stopped us from breathing. We could not cough, sneeze, nor make any noise because of the hollow sound of the tunnel. If we did, it would make us too easy a target. Our bodies were deep in the sewage so all we could do was think. We could see only tears in each others' eyes with the little lights coming through the cracks, but no one even whispered a complaint. It seemed like an hour later when Fane let us know that we could get out now. We managed to push up the manhole cover and found ourselves in a parking lot.

We smelled terrible but saw no place to wash ourselves. We hated to think how long we'd be in this dreadful condition. Our only light came from the moon. We were disoriented, too. Fane was the toughest of us all. He took the lead in dangerous situations. He searched between the cars in the parking lot and spotted a loose hose in a backyard. He crawled on his stomach under the barbed wire toward the faucet. When he got the water running, he dragged the hose toward us. We could see only his shadow in the complete silence of the night.

Our hopes were crushed when we discovered the hose was too short to reach us. Fane crawled back through the mud and freed the hose, which was caught around an old truck tire. By the time he got back it was impossible to recognize even his face, he was so covered in mud. He managed to stick the hose through the fence. It took about half an hour to clean ourselves off so that we could stand the smell of each other. We did this lying down so no one would even see our shadows. After that we started walking in the cold night air so our clothes would dry by morning.

We jumped a few more fences then found a plum tree and an apple tree. We limited our time there and got on the road. We walked, wet to the skin, with the night getting continuously colder and colder. So far not one of us got sick so Emil started pushing us to get to the border before daylight.

While we walked through the water of the tunnel, I lost one shoe. There was no way to find it and so I continued without it. When my foot got sore from stones and cuts, I said to Emil, "I have to stop."

He said, "No way!"

"I cut my foot on something."

He examined it. "We can't do anything until daylight."

Fane had an idea. "You don't need long pants. You could wear short ones."

He ripped off the pant legs from the knee down and bandaged my foot with the cloth.

After many stops to rest, we hid in the bushes for the rest of the night. We looked like escapees from the law.

When morning came, we swam across a river to shorten our trip. We did this fully clothed with shoes and all. Fane found some rope and tied us together in a chain so no one could get lost. When we finally got across the temperature was warmer, and we managed to dry our clothes. We felt clean and renewed in spirit.

Our number one concern was if we could make it two more days without food. We had no money left. Each of us was exhausted and starving. It was difficult to keep walking. Our energy was very close to an end. Emil reminded us that we were free to go back to the Communists, who would break us down for the rest of our lives. Our pace was down from 30 kilometers to 10 kilometers a day. Although we were desperately tired, hungry, and weak to the point of exhaustion, we pushed on.

We walked until about 1 p.m., when we started to get heat exhaustion. Emil made the decision to conserve our energy and find a cool place in the woods to sleep all day. We awoke hours later feeling much better and with our energy renewed.

We mentally prepared ourselves for another night of walking through the woods. Before darkness fell, Fane spotted a place which appeared to be a food store and a gas station in the middle of nowhere. We carefully approached and as always Fane left us to check things out for our safety.

The buildings looked like a ghost town, both strange and weird. It was past sunset and getting dark. Emil gave us a sign to come forward to where he stood. Then he turned to us and asked us to sit down.

"Is anyone hungry?" He asked. We were so weak we couldn't answer. Then he asked which of us looked the best dressed. We wondered what the questions were about.

Victor asked, "Fane, are you going crazy?"

"Yes."

He took his shoe off, pulled his smelly sock off, stuck his hand into the sock and brought out a piece of paper that looked like money, a twenty-dollar bill!

He said to Emil, "Since you look the best, take the twenty dollars and go inside and buy some food.

Emil spent only fourteen dollars for all of us including the drinks. He told us to eat very slowly because otherwise we would get sick, and we still had another 24 hours of walking ahead of us. While we ate, he told us that he saw a flashlight and a pair of galoshes that would help me walk better. Everyone agreed that he should go and get them. Immediately we felt brighter and each of us gave a big hug to our friend Fane, who saved our lives in our moment of despair.

We got up and got going again. We walked almost all night into the forest, going higher and higher into the mountains. We heard no sound of any kind in the quiet and dark. The moon hardly peeked through the trees.

When the day started to break, we arrived at a flat grassy area. We thought it would be the best place to rest. After about an hour talking about our journey, we heard the noise of a car. Everyone tried to figure out from which direction it came. We went in the direction we thought was the way to the road. The car went right by us, and no other car came by for a very long time.

We could see the road but were afraid to get too close. We tried to identify the license plate. Then another car came, this time a little brown van with white letters on the top. We realized we were in Italy and the car was a police car. It read "Carabinieri." It is impossible to explain the joy we felt to know that we had arrived in Italy and were essentially safe.

We managed to cross to the other side of the road and hid in a ditch since we were afraid to be mistaken for prison escapees. We looked so bad, dirty, smelly, ragged, and unshaven, that we feared what would happen if someone saw us. Many cars went by, but we waited for another police car.

After a while we saw in the distance another car that looked like a police minivan. Everybody said that I must be the one to wave and ask for help because I was the one who could speak Italian. I remember that I had to make a big effort because I had trouble getting up once I lay down. We were exhausted. When the van got closer, we realized that it was a Carabinieri! In the moment the van got close I got up on my knees and stuck my hand out of the trench and screamed to the top of my lungs. "Aiuto! Aiuto!"

Help! Help!

The van had been traveling fast and continued for about 100 yards and then stopped. Both doors opened and the policemen called out, "Ceh suceso?"

What happened? I repeatedly said, "We need help!" The driver backed up the van and pulled along side of us on the road.

They stared at us in disbelief because we looked so miserable.

I said, "We are Romanians! We need help."

In minutes they realized that we had escaped and needed first aid and protection. When they opened the van's sliding door, they shouted "Die Forze, Forza." Let's go, let's go!

When they saw that we were too weak to move, they loaded us in the back of the van like sacks of potatoes. We heard them talking about our bad smell as they opened their windows. We were too weak to care.

They took us directly to a hospital in Trieste where we were half-carried in and set down. We showered and put on clean clothes. Then the doctors carefully examined each of us and treated us for malnutrition and dehydration. It took us about two weeks to recover in the hospital until we were able to walk on our own, again. They gave us each 25,000 lire (about $15), and a place to sleep in a nearby pensione until the next day.

Chapter Sixteen:
On our Way to Freedom

From then on, our lives began to evolve into a more normal way of living. We felt great relief to be on the road to recovery and that our days of existing on wild fruits from the trees and managing without water for about eighteen hours were behind us. They fed us and told us that we would be in danger in the streets. Even if we were not totally free from troubles, we looked at each other and could not keep from smiling.

Later, the police advised us that we must be very careful and aware when we walked around town without protection. Without knowing how it took place, we could find ourselves back in Romania.

They recommended that we stick around in the pensione until they could take us to the refugee camp for interrogation. The interrogation, once we got to the camp, consisted of identification information, such as name, country, and date of birth. The information was then sent to Interpol to make sure we were the people we claimed to be.

In the morning they took us to the downtown area where we could apply for political asylum. After three days in the pensione, we went to a small village high in the mountains named Padriciano. This place looked like a POW camp. About 400 refugees lived there. They didn't allow us to leave the compound, so we spent time hanging around listening to music on the radio. I recall the chapel was open 24 hours every day. We could only go to the city in groups and needed to have our own money. In approximately six weeks, our papers were ready, and we were divided into groups for relocation in different parts of Italy. Refugees were sent to one of two places, Latina, near Rome, and Capua, near Naples. Victor and Fane were sent to Latina. Emil and I were sent to Capua.

After we settled into the refugee camp, they gave us folding metal beds with straw mattresses which we carried from the storage area inside the camp. We stayed in old WW II cabins. The rooms included either two or three beds. The bath was at the end of the hallway and the toilets were holes in the floor with a tank of water high on the wall and a rope or chain to pull for washing down after each use.

In the beginning it felt like a desperate situation. Everyone talked about how it could take six months to a year to emigrate. For the United States the time was indefinite. A person's name went on a list. Someone then had to pick out your name and sponsor you. Many people sat in the camp for more than two years with no hope. I looked at this and thought I had plenty of time before I got sponsored, time for me to make plans until someone sponsored me.

My friend, Emil, took his drawing board to downtown Capua, a very old town with architecture from ancient Roman times. He sketched buildings, which used up time as he waited every day for an answer. He relaxed in this way along with the pleasure of some Italian wine.

I found a job in the nearest town, Caserta, as a mechanic working on Italian cars. It was a short bus ride away and for a short time I did this until someone accepted me as a second driver on a semi-truck. This job kept me busy but away from my friends, who I missed, and the pay was not very good. So, I went back to look for a job nearby which would be more convenient if my name were picked up. Then, too, when together, we kept up each others' spirits.

When I got back, I looked for Emil to check on how his spirit held up. After more than a year, no one had yet sponsored us.

I rushed to downtown Capua and questioned everyone about the Romanian painter. Someone sent me to the corner where the old Roman road began. I found him in a small house in ruins, where he was finishing his drawing of the ruins that were part of the old Via Appia. This was the half-mile piece of road that remained from the time of the Romans.

I was amazed at what he could do. It was getting late so I helped him gather up his supplies and we went back to the refugee camp. We took time to clean up for the evening to go to a movie that had been set up for us. That night they were playing the movie *MacArthur* with George C. Scott. Everyone was anxious to see it and we wanted to get a good seat. After we saw the movie, we became even more excited about becoming a part of this great country.

The next day in the morning, we met in the line waiting for coffee and a small breakfast. He told me he had an idea and wanted to go to my room where we could talk. As soon as we sat down, he told me a story he had never told us before. He said he was a married man with two children in Romania. In that moment, I realized that leaving his wife and family was such a big sacrifice that mine didn't seem to compare. He sacrificed his life for his family, never knowing if he would see them again. Overnight, I became stronger in my belief that I would, one day, be an American. Days went by and we met more Romanians but only Emil and I were from the capital,

Bucharest. Many rough guys hung around there and a few knew a lot about how to make things happen. Two days later, they took us into the town, and we found a guy who needed people to load semi-trucks with mineral water. We needed the money and took the job. We found the owners to be rough and mean people who allowed no time for breaks. They used us as though we were their property and totally ignored giving us any human respect or dignity.

That night these guys said they had a better idea. We should go to Napoli and change our identity. We could get a passport and a driver's license so we could go to Germany. Two days later my name was Pietro Paulo Mauritzio, who lived in Rome, Italy. Now I could go to Germany. My goal was to go to Frankfurt with my new friends, leaving Emil behind in the camp where he had found a job in the office and the infirmary.

As soon I got there, I would enter my name on the list at the US Air Base for volunteer work at the loading dock.

We found two more guys interested in also doing this. We packed our few things and took off for a long, cramped journey in a very small 600 Fiat. We left on Friday morning and got to Frankfurt on Sunday, driving straight through. On Monday morning we cleaned up at the home of a friend of this guy with all the connections. We got to the place to sign up, we each had to go through a one-hour interview. They asked us to fill out a questionnaire, the first time in my life I had to fill out an application in English. It seemed that each day I was progressing in the right direction.

They told us to wait for a week for an answer. We left the number of the friend's house and returned there. That night he took us to a restaurant, and we started to wash dishes so we could survive while we awaited the phone call.

Not more than two days later we received a call. We dropped everything, jumped in the car, and made our way there as soon as we could. When we got there, we saw more people lined up from the gate to the office.

We gave our names and joined the group. Everybody tried to do the best they could and marched to the main warehouse. Here we were briefed about what jobs we were assigned to. They told us where we were allowed to be on the base and where we were not allowed. Some of us had to be trained for our jobs.

I was asked to operate a forklift because of my experience. Listening to the American personnel, I thought that I would never learn English, but I was still very excited to be among them. Soon after we were told where to go to pick up our work uniforms, which were not much different from theirs except that we had no names on our shirts. I remember when I went into the dressing room and picked them up and put them on. I turned around and looked in the mirror. I could not believe what I saw.

The joy in my eyes was indescribable. Tears of joy came from remembering that not long ago I was not sure if I would live or die before becoming a free man. On the left side of my shirt a patch said a few great words, "US Air Force!"

My mind went straight back home to my family, thinking that I wished they could see me. I was happy but sad that I could not share this with my family.

A fellow from Poland, Marek, who knew a little English, also worked there. He spoke to the Air Force personnel and he and I conversed in Italian. I even picked up a few words of English that helped me when I later got to the United States. Every night I fell asleep thinking of what would happen next and how I would find my way to America. Each day when I got dressed, I touched myself and my new uniform, finding it hard to believe this was really me.

Two weeks later I completed my training as a forklift operator. I felt proud to perform my responsibilities and felt like the best forklift operator ever. Six months went by quickly. After I seriously injured my ankle in a loading accident, I had to have medical assistance and was hospitalized for surgery on my damaged ankle. After about a month, I started to walk and although I was not up to working yet I was ready to go back to Italy. The doctors told me it would be better to go somewhere for a period of rest.

I called a good friend in Italy and learned that my name had come up on a list for going to the USA. They said that a priest from the Romanian Orthodox Church in New York City had sponsored me, and it was very possible that I could be leaving soon with the first group in January 1970.

When I heard that, the whole world came down on top of me. After I hung up, I was full of new plans. With the little money I made during this time working, I bought some heavy clothing from Germany because I heard that New York in January was very cold.

The next day I began my effort to find a way to get back to Italy. Once again, the friend helped me to make my way by train.

Every moment after my return to Italy, I had the sensation that every minute was one hour, and every hour was one day.

While I was gone, my friend, Emil, with the help from the Italian government and the United Nations was about to go to a special university in Bologna, Italy and take his certification so he could practice medicine anywhere in the world. I wish I could have said goodbye to him, but I knew he would come to New York in the summer.

With the group that would depart together, we celebrated Christmas and had a joyous holiday full of expectations. I went to Rome for one last trip, thinking that I would never be able to visit there again.

The days went quickly by and on January 11, I found myself in a moment of truth as I boarded the Pan American 707. I was going to realize the dream that I had for so many, many years. I, Cornell Iliescu, was going to America to face new challenges and new customs where the leaders of freedom would give me a new way of life. My dream was coming true!

Chapter Seventeen: Touchdown on US Soil

The moment the airplane came to a stop, I had no words to describe my feelings. When I descended the ladder from the 707, I thought of having waited for this since I was a little boy of 7.

Everything happened fast after I went through customs. I soon found myself standing in front of the airport with a small suitcase and an umbrella. Three more Romanians waited there for the rest of the group to get on the bus. I looked around. It felt like I was in a dream or a movie from the past.

After about a half hour we arrived in Downtown Manhattan at the Walcott Hotel, an old building right next to the Empire State building that dated from 1902 and was famous during the 20's and 30's. In the lobby of the hotel all the awaiting Romanians seemed happy to see more of their countrymen coming to the USA.

After long hours of flying, I felt tired, so I went to my room. It was a lot for me to take in. Two other guys shared the room with me. The first thing they told me was we might have overnight visitors.

"Who might they be," I asked.

One of them said, "We had some mice or rats climbing in the bed in the night looking for food."

I figured they were kidding, but soon learned they were not. For the first two nights, I had no trouble sleeping yet I kept expecting to feel something.

After a few days, I got a job through someone at the church and once I started working, I forgot about rats.

My friend Victor, who escaped with me and who arrived one month ahead of me, showed up at the hotel. I saw him waiting in the lobby when I came home from work. The minute he saw me, he jumped up from his chair to hug me and I told him to take it easy.

We talked of many things from the past for about a half hour, then he suggested it would be better to move in with him as a roommate. He even offered me a job in home remodeling. I thanked him and reminded him that I had no money. I thought about it for two days and decided that it was better to be with someone I knew than to be alone.

The next day I called him and asked when I could move in. He picked me up and we took the subway to 42nd Street in Queens, New York.

We walked around the area and found a lot of furniture available on the street and even a beautiful rug. It seemed too good to be true. Soon everything looked homey and nice. At first, I had to sleep on the floor but the next day we went out and found a very nice sofa to sleep on.

It took only about a week to realize that this situation was not working to my advantage. I worked every day but had no money. Victor's standard answer to when I would get paid was, "Next week."

Then he said I talked too much on the phone to my dad and when he deducted the charges, there was no money for me. He, however, spent lots of money at the bar and playing pool in the evenings. This went on for about two months until my savings from Italy were almost gone. In the end, I had twenty-five dollars left.

One evening he sat with me at the table. He said that he needed to tell me something important.

He said to me in no uncertain terms, "You must move out because Zoie, my girlfriend, is moving in with me. She is moving in tonight and you must go, now."

For a moment I was in a state of shock and didn't ask "Where am I to go?" When reality struck me, I asked where he would suggest I go.

He replied, "It's not my business but first I must tell you that you owe me money and I am going to keep your belongings here until you pay me $300."

Minutes later I found myself walking on the street with no place to go. The weather in March was cold, so I had to find a place to keep warm. I was all alone with no friends and no one to talk to. I remembered that I had a phone number of a friend from the refugee camp in Italy. He was very nice and offered to come and pick me up at the subway station. We went to his house and talked about our journey to America.

I was too embarrassed to tell him my problem. He offered to go for a bite to eat. The time went quickly and at about 11 p.m. I had to leave.

At first, I planned to get on the bus, but I changed my mind and went into the subway. I spent two weeks in the subway, sleeping all night there. I met some other homeless guys, and we struck up a friendship.

On the first day one of them asked me for a quarter. I had no idea what quarter meant. The next time I saw the priest, I told him my story and asked him what quarter meant. He said,

"Son, this is a funny story." He explained how the money system works. I then knew what a quarter was.

He also said to come and see him at the office because he might be able to find me another job where I could be a mechanic without owning my own tools.

When next I saw my friend, he again asked if I had a quarter. This time I said, "sure" and gave him one. He refused the quarter and gave me a hug and said that now we were "buddies."

After two weeks on the subway, Easter Sunday arrived, and I went to church. A lot of people gathered in front of the church, talking, enjoying the day, and breaking the Easter eggs with each other as is the custom.

When I arrived, I met some guys I remembered from Italy. I never mentioned being homeless and we talked. I got a few ideas about work. Suddenly, a guy who looked familiar walked towards me and called my name. He hugged me and asked me how in the world I got to America and where was my brother.

I explained as briefly as possible because more people surrounded me. They said they'd known me since I was a little kid. Turned out these were his father, mother, and the whole family.

When they asked where I lived and where I worked, I tried to avoid answering but they asked repeatedly. I finally had to tell them my problems.

His father said, "This is not a problem. From now on you will stay with us!"

He called his son Romi and gave him $300 cash, the amount I supposedly owed to Victor.

He said, "Don't waste any more time. Go pick up his belongings and bring them to our house."

They took me to their car. We drove to Victor's apartment. Romi went in and told Victor he was paying the money and wanted to pick up my things.

From Queens, New York, we drove all the way to the Bronx to the man's father's apartment, where I met his 98-year-old grandma. They suggested that I watch her during the day. Later in the afternoon, when others came home, I could look for my job.

Grandma was a nice lady but a little forgetful. My life changed on the spot. I now had my own room and my own shower. I took time to write home and explain to my family that a new life in a new country was not as easy as I thought it would be.

One evening when I went out, I met some other Romanian guys who had been in the country for a while. One told me he intended to quit his job at a Texaco gas station and asked if I would like to take his place. He said I might have to do a lot of pumping gas on the island before they would trust me to do mechanic's work.

It did not take very long before their broken Italian/Sicilian language helped me communicate with them and I picked up a little English. I started to work hard, including a lot of overtime to make money so I could rent my own room and live closer to work.

Soon my first year passed and my English improved so I could get a better job. After working two years, a customer said, "Cornell, you don't belong here. I have a better job for you."

I started with earnings of $1.86/hour and after two years I was making $2.25/hour. I couldn't complain because I needed the job. I was also afraid that my English was not good enough for me to be on my own.

My customer, who was a driver for the CEO of The Bank of America, filled up the big Cadillac he drove almost every day. He often asked when I would come to work with him and give up my current job.

By this time, I owned my own tools and my rolling bench. I could fix almost any car. I also saved money to buy my own car, a 1966 Oldsmobile Delta 88.

Every day I saw how my life changed for the better, but I needed a little more courage to risk it all for a better job. I was afraid to tell my boss I wanted to quit because I wasn't sure if I would succeed.

One day, my driver friend, Jim, told my boss that they wanted to invite me to lunch. He took me a short distance away to an Oldsmobile dealer where he introduced me to the manager.

He said to him, "This is the man I was talking about. He is very talented. You will be happy to have him on your team."

The manager handed me an application and Jim helped me fill it out. The next week, I took two days off from my old job so I could work part time as a test for the new job. I had to write my own work orders and ask in English for the parts I needed. I realized then that my confidence in my command of English had grown. No one could stop me now.

On the next Sunday, I went to the Romanian church and talked to the priest. He mentioned a man who was married and had small children. He worked as a truck driver in Romania. He was desperate and very happy to apply for the job I was leaving."

The next day, when I went back to my old job, it seemed like my boss had some bad feelings. He asked me directly, "Do you want to quit? If so, I want you to find a replacement before you leave."

Since I didn't know any mechanics, I said, "I'm not sure I can do that. However, I will stay for the time being."

He immediately said he would raise my salary to $2.50 per hour just to stay. I agreed to reconsider.

Two weeks later I received a call from the dealer that they accepted me and could I start working immediately. My starting salary was $5.00 per hour and this I could not refuse. I was very happy. My English was better, and no one could stop me now.

Six months went by, and I was doing great! Then one day when I came home a little late, I opened my door and a terrible mess met my eyes. Everything was torn apart and upside down. I heard about homes being broken into, but I never thought it could happen to me. I'd been robbed. Every small thing of value was gone as if the person who did this job knew exactly where I put my precious things.

Cash seemed to be the main objective. They thought I probably kept my money at home. I did, however, have a bank account since I met Jim, the driver. He took me to the bank to set it up.

First, I grabbed the phone to make a call, but the line was dead. I wanted to call some friends to tell them what happened to me. I had to walk down the street to a liquor store and call from the public phone. The only thing they said was, "I'm sorry."

My windows were broken, and I was on the ground floor, so I called the manager where I worked and explained what happened. He said I could sleep at his house. The next day I took a day off from work and paid the balance of rent on my small apartment. I took some things from my place and went to see my friend Nick in Parsippany, New Jersey. He was supposed to be a good friend since we'd known each other since elementary school. We had both lost contact for about 15 years until we met again in the refugee camp in Italy. He was married with a wife and two daughters.

It looked like he was happy to have me around. He offered to let me stay in the kitchen where he had a bed. Things were fine except that I had a longer commute to my job and lost an additional hour of sleep in the morning and another hour at the end of the day.

Two months went by. Nick began to drink a lot and started to be sarcastic and to make nonsense jokes that were not funny at all. In the end he became very nasty.

In the meantime, one Sunday, when I was walking in downtown Dover, New Jersey, I met a person in a store. He noticed me reading a "Room for Rent" sign on the door and approached me. He asked me if I needed a room. I replied that I did. After we exchanged a few words, he noticed my accent and asked me where I was from. When I told him I was from Romania, he called out to tell his wife to come and meet me.

He said, "Here is another Romanian. My cousin in Italy is married to a Romanian girl and they are very happy."

He then proceeded to offer me the room for $95/month, which was very cheap. I also had access to the whole house. That evening, when I returned to Nick's house, he invited me to eat with them. Another guest was there, too, so I could not talk to him alone. When we talked the following day, I told him I was moving out. He said that it would be better to be on my own but acted as if he were about to lose a friend.

At the beginning of my third year in this country, things went well until one day I had a surprise visit from Nick along with Victor from New York. Victor wanted to apologize for everything he did to me and wanted to make it up to me. Together they invited me to Victor's home in Queens, New York. He said he had broken up with Zoie and was alone again. He wanted to talk about a new plan of his that would be good for both of us. I said I would think about getting together but I would never step foot in his apartment again.

My curiosity led me to ask Nick about Victor's plans. He said he didn't know. When I said that I must get back to work, Victor apologized all over again and repeated how important it was that we meet. During the period when we hadn't seen each other, he had traveled to California several times. He met some people especially a lady, Maria Ravaru, who had been a ballerina at the Variety (like our Broadway) in Romania. She was in her sixties.

Victor was trying to get away from Zoie Cimpeanu because he owed her some money. Everything he proposed had nothing to do with me. He needed someone with a car who could tow a trailer and help him move to Los Angeles. To lure me he talked about the wonderful weather in southern California and about what a beneficial effect it would have on my lifelong migraines.

After about an hour of talking, we ended our discussion with me no closer to a decision. I felt my interest growing yet didn't want to trust him again. I knew the hot humid summer was horrible for my headaches, and I wasn't looking forward to suffering that again. Then, too, whether I trusted him or not it would be convenient to be with someone who knew his way around California. I felt myself leaning in that direction and said I would do it. By the end of July, I was on my way to California. It took us three and a half days to get to Hollywood.

During our trip he continually asked me for money for the cold beers he enjoyed and for big breakfasts. He never wanted to taste any of the sandwiches I put in the cooler nor any of the fruit I brought.

He finished the beers and was always ready for more at every stop. I thought to myself that I would be wise to lend him an amount that he could repay so I gave him $400. I told him I'd keep $100 for myself plus $180 for gasoline. I knew he didn't believe that it was all the money I had, but we continued to Los Angeles. I focused on getting to a place where I could put my head down.

On the third day in the afternoon at about 3 p.m. we reached Hollywood. He took me straight to his friend, Mary, who was happy to see us. We stayed up late eating and talking about our trip.

Mary offered to call some people so I could work on a few cars while waiting until I found a job. She said that for the time being, I could stay in the guesthouse on her property. This made me happy because it was nice and clean and a good start for me.

She kept me busy for a while working on cars. One day she received a call from a friend who owned an Arco Gas Station in North Hollywood. The next day she drove me there to meet the owner. After a short interview, he told me to bring my tools and get started immediately.

After only three days working there, the owner took off for Las Vegas and I was alone in charge of everything. It seemed like he was happy I could take care of his business. It was quite a big responsibility for me at a rate of pay no more than I was getting on the East Coast.

My life again went in a new direction although a difficult one. My boss gave me confidence and he was happy with the profit he made on me, sometimes 13 hours a day for a flat $200/week.

My main goal was to keep away from Victor. I waited for an apartment to come available next to the gas station. The owner of the apartment expected one in two weeks. I went home that evening, told Mary, and asked her to allow me to stay two more weeks. I would pay her. She agreed but said I needn't pay because I did a great job on her car, and she was very happy with it. Victor did not want to lose contact with me because he needed a driver and someone to open doors for him. He never mentioned the $400 he owed me in the two months after our arrival in California even though he worked full time remodeling and painting homes.

The next Sunday he decided to visit a friend who I also knew from the refugee camp in Italy. Victor talked to him, and he said he wanted to see me. When I walked in the door, I saw a very poor apartment with almost no furniture, just a couch and cocktail table and the kitchen in the same room.

He watched TV and, in the corner, a young lady from Columbia, Yadira, sat quietly. She later offered us a cup of coffee.

During the entire visit she never exchanged a word with us but sat there and listened to us talk. When we left, I put my business card on the table. A few days later, she showed up at my work with a pair of tail lenses for her car since someone backed into hers. I gladly offered to replace them for her. I invited her into the office and went out to get her some coffee.

While I worked on the car, she moved close to me and told me the problems she had with her Romanian boyfriend. He drank and gambled in Las Vegas and treated her poorly. He gambled away his money and called her to drive to Las Vegas to pick him up.

She asked me, "Would you tell him on the phone in Romanian that I would break up with him if he didn't change?"

I said, "He has an addiction that won't go away. You are wasting your time."

She said, "The last time he left, he didn't show up for two weeks and I had to go back to my grandmother's home."

About two weeks later, Yadira showed up again at my gas station with her girlfriend, Maite, who surprised me by saying she knew my boss and had work done there on her car before.

Before Yadira left with Maite, we talked about meeting sometime outside of work. She told me she was living with her grandmother now. We became good friends.

I asked her, "Do you knew any places to go and dance?"

She said, "Of course. I will call you this weekend to tell you where to meet me."

We started meeting more often. She seemed to enjoy my company. One month later I invited her to my new apartment in Hollywood. I said I would cook some Romanian dinner if she would like to join me. We had a great night. She liked the dinner very much and even helped me wash the dishes. We talked a lot about ourselves. I invited her to spend the night with me.

At first, she said, "Yes" then changed her mind because she said her grandmother would be worried. I drove her home and met her grandmother, who seemed happy to meet me. We said goodbye with the intention that we would see each other again.

Two weeks went by. I never heard from her. I worried that I offended her because I asked her to spend the night with me.

Having nothing to do on weekends, I spent time sprucing up my apartment. I started by cleaning the spots on the carpet, which were there when I moved in. I scrubbed on my hands and knees, then left the door open so the carpet would dry faster. When I got closer to the door, I saw two small feet on my doorstep. It was Yadira, my little Columbian friend, watching me work.

I said, "Where'd you come from?"

She said, "I've been watching you for a time and waited for you to be surprised but you never looked up. Why didn't you respond to my letter?"

"I never received a letter."

"I put it under your door almost two weeks ago."

We both closed the door and found the letter sitting in the corner behind the door. From that minute I knew she had feelings for me. We both enjoyed the moment and laughed together.

I invited her in and asked her to sit down and join me in a cup of tea. We sat together and read the letter. In the letter, she said she wanted to know more about me. She wanted to spend more time together. I couldn't believe the good news. I was very happy to hear it. After getting her something to eat, I showered. We went out and then spent that night together and from that night on.

Two or three months went by. I met the rest of her family, and we spent a lot of time with them. One day she came home from school and told me that her student visa was about to expire. She would have to go back to Columbia.

This shocked me. I was very attached to her and could not see myself alone again. We had a long talk, and I explained my feelings to her. "I don't think I would be happy without you."

She said, "I have no choice. I can't stay here without a visa."

I said, "I have a better idea. I want you to marry me. You won't have to work. We will have a family and you can stay home and care for the children."

She smiled and said, "I will have to call my mother."

She gave her mother the news and from then on, we started looking for a new bed and better furniture. Before long we moved to the apartment which became available next to the gas station. The news spread quickly among friends and family, including my family in Romania. Life took a huge turn. Dreams came true.

We started arrangements for our wedding at the Romanian Church in Glendale to be held a few weeks later. Our friends, including Mary, all offered to help, so each had a little job to do. We put together a nice affair, quickly, and left for our honeymoon in Tahoe, Yosemite, and Las Vegas. Each day that went by I thought how happy I was. I finally found a person to be with for the rest of my life. I truly had "my love to keep me warm."

I became a married man with many friends to do things with and a lot of future plans. I enjoyed life. It was close to the end of 1975 and Christmas was just around the corner. Our expenses doubled so I had to work overtime at people's homes during weekends to keep up.

My boss started to show his anger. Now as a married man, I was not at his disposal every day. One day I told him, "I've worked for you for two years and think I deserve a raise."

His response was very quick. "You're not working as hard as earlier now that you're married. You go home early on Saturdays and on Sundays you don't work."

This wasn't true but he seemed to be trying to put me down as being undeserving of a raise. From then on, I was not the same person. My mind started to be preoccupied with survival. His mind was on how to get richer without spending any money.

Then my brother in Romania accused me of betraying him by getting married before I brought him and his family to the US. I guess he thought that I was very rich after five years in America. He got to the point of threatening me. "You will pay dearly when I get there."

Things were getting tougher and tougher for me.

Despite all the pressure, we enjoyed a great Christmas with family and friends. Then at the beginning of January, my wife went in for a physical. A nearby uncle accompanied her there. When she returned, she told me, "We are going to have a baby."

She was pregnant one month! Everything from that moment took on a new light. We both felt more responsible now in addition to our joy. Once again, dreams turned into reality.

We decided that she would watch every penny because we needed to pay for our medical insurance. We sat on a barrel ready to explode. I told my boss that either I would get a raise, or I would have to look elsewhere, perhaps at a Fiat dealer.

I started to look around and found that a Fiat/Volvo dealer on Ventura Boulevard in Studio City needed a mechanic and found a Fiat shop that needed a Fiat specialist. If my boss fired me, I wouldn't have a problem.

The following day, I asked my boss for a fifty dollar raise. We talked for about an hour before he consented. For him it was a drop in the bucket because he could go through that in a few minutes in Las Vegas and not regret it. To me it was a life saver.

At the same time, my brother was getting closer and closer to getting his visa to go to Italy. In the meantime, his wife was able to smuggle the kids to Switzerland through the help of a doctor friend of mine. My brother called to say that I had to pay for the airline ticket for him to go to Italy. My wife told me to do this we had to apply for a credit card. "You must help your brother," she said.

I worked late every day. One day, when I was working late, a few minutes before I planned to go home to my wife, who was now six months pregnant, an old car pulled into the island and an old lady stepped out and asked for water since her car was overheating badly.

As I popped the hood, I heard a hissing sound. All the lights were off, so I used my flashlight to try to locate the leak. Moments later the radiator exploded. Gallons of hot boiling water filled with antifreeze hit me under my arm and all over the side of my body.

Luckily, a good friend of mine who was waiting for me to close the shop since he was coming to the house for dinner, saw what happened. He rushed next door to my apartment and told my wife. She rushed over and when she saw me, she called 911. When the fire paramedics arrived, they said I was lucky that my arm protected my face. They transported me to a burn hospital in Van Nuys which treated firemen because I had second degree burns.

That was just what I needed. Now I couldn't work for who knew how long. A week later my boss called to say I needed to get back to work or he would hire someone else. My hand had to be elevated so the burn could cure, and the skin could heal properly. I was not able to go back to work.

Two weeks later I received a letter from the insurance company that they would not cover my expenses. The report which my boss submitted said the accident had not occurred during business hours. I had to pay $2,700.

A customer, who did pro bono work as an attorney, heard my story, and volunteered to help me. He guided me to get disability while I healed so I could survive. He threatened to sue the insurance company for many thousands, and they gave in and covered me.

From there on, I knew I had to look for another job but must hang in there for a few more months. After a month, I went back to work. My wound became infected from perspiration and dust. I had to keep it open so I covered it with a special tissue from the burn center. When my boss heard about me getting disability, he was not happy because he said his insurance premium would go higher.

No matter what, my wound healed better every day with the new treatment and the new medications. My wife was now getting close to eight months, and I needed more money. I knew I needed a better job, so I went to the Fiat independent shop, applied, and got the job right away.

On the next Saturday, I removed my tools, took them to the other place, and on Monday morning I dropped off the keys. When the boss took the keys from me, he was very upset and angry. He stepped on my toe and tried to jab a pencil into my stomach. I grabbed the pencil and broke it. He said, "You betrayed me!"

I said, "You live out of my sweat. You've exploited me and you have never appreciated what I have done for you all these years!"

The next week, I started my new job. I worked with some Italian friends I had met before. Now I had a bunch of Italians, Argentines, and English to work with, so I was able to speak the three languages: English, Italian, and Spanish, which was a lot of fun. I was paid better and was happy again in my work.

1976 was a big year with the Bicentennial celebrations. Elvis Presley died. My precious son was born. Now my main concern was our family unit.

My brother left Romania and made it to Italy. He tried to reunite with his wife and children, who were in Switzerland. Finally, through immigration people, he received papers and passports for each one to come to the United States.

I worked for this to happen and now found myself having to come up with four one-way airline tickets to the United States. I talked to my wife again and with help from her aunt we managed to pay for the tickets. In the meantime, knowing he would need a car, I found an old Plymouth Valiant which today would be worth a lot of money. When he saw it later, he accused me of insulting him.

They finally arrived and I tried to help them find an apartment. In the meantime, they slept in my living room. They thought they could stay like that for a while. I knew the landlord would give me notice to move out. Soon that is exactly what happened. When I told my brother what happened, he accused my wife of reporting them to the landlord. When I tried to explain to the landlord, he said he could not give me more than a month.

My brother contacted friends, including Victor, telling them that I brought them to this country and now was throwing them onto the street. Some friends offered blankets because they claimed they had no covers, all of it a lie meant to embarrass us.

Victor, my "best" friend, invited them, behind my back, to come to his apartment for dinner. Then Victor told my brother that I found my wife on the Sunset Strip and that she had been a prostitute.

When my brother returned home, he told me that my wife had been a whore. I was shocked that my brother would say such a disgusting thing. Here I went deeply in debt to bring him here and he treats me like this.

Once again, Victor betrayed me and broke his promise that he would never again betray me. This time he planted seeds of discord between my brother and me that could never be forgotten. Soon after that my brother moved and went to work for a cousin in Costa Mesa, California, and their third son was born.

I had to move out because the landlord refused to allow me to live there anymore. I did have friends in Costa Mesa and started to look for a place there because I thought it might be a better place for us. I also still felt a need to be close to my brother. In spite of all that happened I loved him and felt that he would soon realize how wrong he had been and be sorry. I found it impossible that my brother would believe a stranger and not his own brother.

With a new son being born, I went to congratulate him and let him know that I would be moving to Costa Mesa at the end of the month because the landlord had kicked me out. We were completely broke, with losing my job, my apartment, and having incurred deep debts. I didn't even have the money for my baby's diapers or his milk. Only with the help of my wife's aunt, Nellie, were we able to make the move. Over the next few months we were able to make the move and only with the help again from my wife's aunt were we able to make the move. In the next few months, we did pay back every cent.

I immediately found a job and things began to get better. I met a new friend, Luigi Pellitteri, an Italian, and we became very close. Even our families were close. We worked together at the same dealership as a team. I helped him with his English and his wife helped my wife to cook Italian. My friendship with a stranger was so rewarding that it helped me forget the experiences with so-called friends and with family.

When I thought things were getting back to normal in my life, my little boy started not feeling good. One night we ended up in the Emergency Room at the hospital. We waited for almost an hour.

Finally, the doctor called us in and told us that our son had pneumonia and severe asthma which he would stick with him for the rest of his life. It was heartbreaking to leave him in the hospital and go home without him. For the first time in my life, I asked God what I did wrong. I asked Him to please punish me and not an innocent little child. My wife and I felt alone.

A week later we got him home. He seemed a lot better with the pneumonia but the asthma we would deal with for many years. I spent many a night in the shower holding him in my arms so he could breathe better.

After changing jobs a few times to try to improve my income, I lost interest and thought that I would be better off in my own place. I started to buy, fix up, and sell used cars so I could save the money to rent and start a new business.

I worked for BJ Sports Cars on Harbor Boulevard in Costa Mesa when I made my decision that it would be my last job working for somebody else.

Driving up and down Placentia Avenue in Costa Mesa, I saw a building under construction with a sign "Units for Rent" I went inside and met the owner, Ed Miltonberg.

"I'm interested in a unit for an automotive business," I said.

"No, no, no," he said.

"I have a family, a wife and child. The money I make at the dealership is not enough to support my family.

A young lady with him said, Why don't you come back tomorrow at about 4 p.m."

I felt there was some hope there.

The next day, I went home from work early, took the Vespa and my little son and went to meet the lady who was waiting for me. When she saw us, she came outside and took us to a unit that was almost finished.

"I have an idea," she said. "My husband Ed works hard, and he could use some help."

She pointed to a pile of scrap building materials that needed to go to the dump. "Do you see that pickup truck? You can load it up with all that stuff and take it to the dump!"

The next day, I went there to do what she asked. The owner was surprised when I said what I was doing. "Can you come by every day?"

"I'll do my best to come here every day."

"How much do you want?"

"No charge. I am here to help you."

"Do you think you are going to convince me to rent you a space?"

"It's okay. I will keep looking but most places are too far from where I live."

For about three months, I made trips to the dump and helped to clean up other stuff. In the meantime, we became friends.

One afternoon, I received a phone call from him inviting me to come to his home in the Back Bay area of Newport Beach.

He was waiting on his porch and invited me inside. We sat at a table and then his wife came to the table and started talking to me about my background.

"Where are you from and what's your story?" She asked.

He offered me some refreshments and then took out a folder with an application for rental of a unit.

He helped me fill it out and explained to me what to say when I went to the city planning department.

The city took about a month and a half but finally I was approved.

By late December 1979, I had a limited supply of tools to get started. A friend helped me to make up a flier to attract Fiat owners. I took the Vespa and my three-year-old son Radu helped me to place flyers on every single Fiat we could find on the streets. Not long after we got our first customers.

We began the business that would help us to survive without any help from others. Six months later we had enough money to install a hoist and enough work for another mechanic. We also installed an air compressor, and my wife had her own office. We were full fledged business owners. By 1983 we had two hoists and three mechanics working full-time. By 1984 we had five mechanics, two units, and we were ready to buy two new cars and a home.

In the meantime, we had a second darling boy, Bogdan, born in 1982. We were a very happy little family. It looked like we had realized the American Dream. During this period, I worked on getting my mother to come to be with me. My dear father, Emil, had died in 1973 and things were not easy for her being all alone. She arrived in 1984 and moved in with us in our new house. Here, once more new personal problems faced me.

My brother's family began to tell the old story of my wife, trying to get my mother to believe these unspeakable things. My wife started to take things more seriously. She suggested that it would be better for my mother to move out of the house and live with my brother. I totally agreed. I told my mother she would hush up or move out.

When my brother heard that my mother had to move to his house, he said, "See, I told you and you wouldn't believe me."

My mother went to live with my brother and many years went by without any of us speaking because I wanted to save my marriage. But because they were talking about us to others, my wife and I started to have arguments.

Now, when everything was on the right track with a new home, new cars, new baby, another bombshell had to come and ruin our lives. On May 5th, 1985, my wife filed for divorce. I thought my world was coming to an end. We continued to be friendly and respectful with each other. She still helped me at the shop, but our business was up and down. Fiat stopped importing cars into the USA in 1984 and this affected our business. At this point, instead of her helping me at the shop, I thought it would be better for her to pursue a degree in accounting so she could support herself and the children in case something happened to me. I also did not want her to lose the house which was so dear to me.

I remember when I was a kid the government confiscated our home. We had no home and we lived, the whole family, in two little rooms with no bath, only a toilet. I didn't want my children to live as I did.

The separation between the father and the children was so difficult and stressful that I decided not to sell the home but struggled to pay for it for quite a few years until she could refinance the house and complete the payments. She rented out two rooms to help with the payments. This helped me a lot so I could continue working in my shop. Because things were not going well, I had to one by one let my mechanics go and reduce my space to one unit. I worked all alone on the jobs that came through and was able to pay the rest of the mortgage and my shop rent plus other related business expenses. It was not an easy time in my life. It was very stressful, but I kept the business going.

Chapter Eighteen:
The Divorce bombshell

Even though I knew about the divorce, I always kept in the back of my mind the thought that we would find some way to reconcile and keep the marriage. I tried to appeal to her for the sake of the kids. She did a good job as my assistant at the shop, keeping the books and trying to pay our bills on time. Our business was such that we barely made enough to keep us alive. In the meantime, she went to college to take accounting classes. We made that decision so our kids would have a secure future.

We dragged out the idea of divorce for a few years with me living in the house but not in a very close relationship otherwise. My hope always remained, and I never quit believing that it would somehow all work out. I remember every day I put a fresh flower on the dashboard of her car when she went to work. The only response I got for that was that it was too late. I tried to remind her about how she had been in the same situation as a child and how difficult it was for her to not be in contact with her father then or later in her life. Time went by and nothing improved.

Due to a lack of business, I had to let two of my mechanics go and had to go back to work as a full-time mechanic. In the meantime, she completed her course work at college and continued to work at the shop. Every day it was harder and harder to come up with the mortgage for the house. We had to borrow money from different people, and it became increasingly difficult to pay them back.

I mentioned to her that it might help if she started to look for work elsewhere. She would need to show steady employment to qualify for the loan if she were to assume the payments on the house. It was hard to convince her, but she came to realize that we might otherwise lose the house. After a few temporary jobs she found a permanent job that helped her qualify with the bank to transfer the loan into her name.

Finally, everything was over. We saved the house. She now had the steady job, and with the two rooms rented, she managed to make the payments and survive. The moment I signed the papers and agreed that she would be the sole owner of the house, she told me that from that day on I would not be allowed to come inside the house or to visit my children there. I had to pick them up and take them to where I lived. From that moment, I felt like being the father of her children didn't mean anything to her. I was just another guy.

Among my most painful memories were the holidays, Thanksgiving and Christmas, when I felt so alone and wanted to share this time with my boys. I explained to my older son, 18, how much I wanted to be there with them. He said he would talk to his mother. I was very happy to hear that she agreed if I didn't mind the boyfriend being there. For years to come I struggled to respect her and not show any hate or ill will toward her, especially in front of the children. Yadira was always welcome in my shop and whenever her car needed servicing, I continued to take care of it for thirty years.

After I left my house and lived alone, my mother chose to leave my brother and move back with me. She passed away in 1995. Things got tougher financially, trying to keep up the shop and support the children, too. It became impossible to pay my bills and sadly I filed for bankruptcy. In 1999, my landlord sold the home where I lived, and I was forced to move out.

At this time, I had no place to go, and I was broke. The only option for me was to stay at my shop so I built a little room above my office and created a shower in my restroom which later I paid dearly for because it caused my rent to go up substantially.

In the middle of 1986, I met a lady, Elena, with whom I had a relationship for years. She helped me feel better about myself and in going places with her I included my children with her children. We had fun times together for many years.

Many times, I thought it would be good for us to marry but it was never the right time for her. She helped me in many ways to get through my years of anxiety about the way my life had turned out. Living in the shop was hard on my self esteem, a very low point in my life.

From my family I never had anyone ask how in the world I could live there with the smell of fumes and gas in an unbelievably cold winter.

When I look back now, I feel good that I was able to endure those five years in such a situation without giving up hope. During those years my children grew up. I was always there for them but as with children of divorce, I am not sure they understood what a heartache it was for me to live without them day to day. I was there for them even for small things like rushing to meet them daily to give them their lunch money. I was at every game they played, I encouraged them in their schoolwork, and as much as possible was a part of their lives.

When the time came for them to drive, I made sure they had well serviced cars to drive. I think they have no doubts about what they mean to me and even though the dream was not as I had planned, they turned out to be good kids and I am very proud of them. My older son, Radu, finished his college at UC Santa Barbara and has a good job with the Denso Company.

Radu married a sweet girl, Tatiana, and became the father of a dear grandson, Sage, and a darling little granddaughter, Jasmin. He is a homeowner and a very responsible person.

My younger son, Bogdan, made me very proud when he joined the US Air Force two months before 9/11. He was highly trained as a member of the team that maintained B2 Bombers in Whiteman, Missouri. Soon, however, he became allergic to toxins and left the military to return to school. He graduated from Orange Coast College in Costa Mesa. He is a nature lover with a career in horticulture. He has met a lovely young lady and they have future plans.

In 2020, Cornell, center back, with sos Bogdan. left, and Radu, right, and grandchildren Sage and Jasmine, front.

Chapter Nineteen: Dreams to Come

In the mid 1990s, I had a chance to work on my other dream, which started in the 1940s when I first met my American friends from the B24 Liberator, who inspired me to be an American kid.

In the interim years I joined many Veterans organizations, including the Former POWs Association of Romania, the Freedom Committee of Costa Mesa, the Warbirds Chapter 16 in Chino CA, the Vietnam Veterans of America Chapter 785, and the California Historical Group Living History Association. Many of the members of these groups encouraged me to put my story on paper because it sounded so interesting. They said I should be more involved with passing the torch to the next generation.

In 1996, one of the WWII pilots, Richard Butler, who flew the low-level mission over Romania, invited me to attend a reunion of the 2nd Air Division at the Hyatt Hotel, Irvine, California. They asked me to be one of the guest speakers to talk about my childhood life as an eyewitness to most of the bombing raids from 1943 to 1945 over Ploesti, Romania. They wanted me to share with them what happened to me, how I first tasted chocolate from the hands of the US Airmen, to show them the pliers which were given to me as a toy to keep me quiet, and the small pencil which my mother kept for me in Romania until she came to America in 1983. That invitation and presentation inspired me and gave me the confidence to be more involved with what was happening to the Greatest Generation and what I could do to honor them.

In 1998, the 2nd Air Division again invited me to a big event, this time at their headquarters in Savannah, Georgia, where I was the principal speaker in front of an audience of over a thousand members, family, and honored guests. That day I sent a powerful message to the audience by wearing the uniform of a Veteran who had been one of them. He had retired as a Lieutenant Colonel, and I explained to the people that I was wearing the uniform of this brave man to honor him and to honor them.

I told my complete story and for the first time in my life received a standing ovation. Later, I learned that in the local paper there was an article about a speaker who was an "eyewitness to history." It related that his story brought the audience to its feet for a standing ovation. When one of the members brought the article to me, I recall asking him what they meant by a "standing ovation." The man said that you have been honored by the audience, most of whom were older than 85. They stood up for you and clapped their hands to show their support for you and your dad who with no hesitation chose to risk your lives by saving and hiding downed US Airmen. What happened that day when I finished my speech was even more thrilling because a few Veterans made their way to me and proceeded to tell me that they were the exact guys who had been on the receiving end of my father's heroism in removing them from the wreckage. They also remembered me as a little boy of six to whom one had given a bar of chocolate, one some pliers, and one a pencil.

Years went by. I continued to be a part of the groups which honored the Greatest Generation. Through these groups, I met the most famous pilot of WWII, whose airplane became the most photographed of the time. It appears in any book of photos of WWII.

His name was Major Robert W. Sternfels, and he became one of my best friends. He was the author of *Burning Hitler's Black Gold*. His B-24 Liberator, The Sandman, is part of the famous photo showing the low-level bombing of the Ploesti Oil Refineries. He also volunteered to appear for me in many parades such as the Balboa Island Parade on June 6th and the 4th of July Parade in Huntington Beach.

Starting in 1995 and working with the Veterans groups I began to give my time to participating in patriotic events and in speaking to local school children. I also bought my first WWII Jeep, which I used for parades and other school events. I worked with the AmVets and the American Legion to speak for three days each year to busloads of fifth graders who came to Santa Ana to the Walk of Honor, where they learned about our Medal of Honor recipients.

I told my story each year at high schools which were recording living history about WWII. For many years, during the Christmas season, the Veterans in the Spinal Cord Injury Wing of the VA Hospital in Long Beach were treated to a BBQ and a show which we put on for them where we provided gift bags of goodies to them and to other VA Hospital patients from Orange County to San Diego.

On 9/11 I stood on the streets of Costa Mesa and Huntington Beach in a WWII combat uniform, waved a large American flag, and asked passing cars to honk their horns to honor our country. I also had a WWII flag in my other hand and the anger in me helped me to not mind the weight of the flags until my hands went numb.

Cornell in the 2016 Balboa Island Parade with the Harmonettes

We participated in the nationally televised Huntington Beach 4th of July Parade for many years. The high point of this event was when I was honored to drive Staff Sergeant Walter D. Ehlers, our local Medal of Honor recipient and the last surviving soldier from D-Day, June 6, 1944. I repeated this honor several more times when I was chosen to be his driver at other patriotic events.

For 24 years, we have been a proud part of the Balboa Island Parade in Newport Beach, California. It started with us bringing military vehicles with honored Veterans aboard. Since 2005, instead of just driving the military vehicles in the parades, it seemed more fun and more exciting to see how our GIs came back from war and enjoyed being here dancing with the girls at the Stage Door Canteens. Since then, we have always had dancers in vintage authentic military uniforms or 40's style dresses. The Harmonettes from Vista, California was a huge hit with their nostalgic portrayal of the Andrews Sisters singing their famous WWII songs in perfect harmony. Our group receives a wildly enthusiastic response from this patriotic crowd, who are inspired to scream and shout, "USA! USA!" as we pass! Because of this, year after year we have received many trophies for our entries. It's always a joy for us.

In addition to this activity, since about 1997 I have helped the Veterans who maintained the decommissioned merchant liberty ship, the SS Lane Victory, which was used to make WWII history come alive and to honor deceased merchant mariners through day-long cruises from San Pedro, California to Catalina Island during the summer. I entertained them in several capacities, including dancing, once again with swing and tap dancers but this time with the Harmonettes appearing as the Andrews Sisters. The guests on the ship loved it and although it was a grueling couple of days, the profits kept the ship going and was well worth it.

Cornell and Helen Nielsen dancing in the 2010 Balboa Island Parade

Having made the Veterans my number one priority from day one and dedicating my life to them, I felt the need to honor the approximately 3,000 young men who were missing in action during the three years of bombing raids over the Ploesti oil fields in my country. Therefore, in 2007, I created the nonprofit corporation called The Noble Cause Foundation, a tribute to those fallen heroes who did so much by sacrificing their lives for freedom. The goal has been to build a monument in their honor.

This photo was taken during my dad's visit to the Prisoner of War Camp in Bucharest, Romania, in late 1944, by First Lieutenant Jack Ferris, of Orange County, CA.

My dad came to say goodbye to most of them whom he had rescued during the bombing raids.

The picture was given to me 52 years later by Jack after my Chocolate Story Presentation at the Bombers Breakfast at Coco's Restaurant, Fashion Island, Newport Beach.

Jack Ferris is in the front row with white scarf.

My dear Dad

In 2008, I was nominated by the Freedoms Foundation of Valley Forge, Pennsylvania for my community service to Veterans. I received the George Washington Honor Medal at a special dinner. It is the greatest honor I have ever received.

The Noble Cause Foundation originated because of a desire to honor our Veterans. It began as a seed that was planted over 27 years ago when we started to collect and restore military vehicles for reenactment of WWII battles. As time went on, we needed to use these vehicles to carry our Veterans to the parades. Before long we began to receive numerous requests from civic and Veterans organizations to use these vehicles.

Distinguished Flying Cross recipient, Jack Ferris, hero of Ploesti bombing raids Aug. 1, 1943, with, from left, Kyle Brandse, Cornell, Ferris, and Nicholas Dimancescu.

This endeavor made it possible to increase the exposure of our Veterans to the public, thus creating more opportunities for them to be recognized for their service and for the sacrifices they made for our freedom.

There was one special battle for the most strategic targets during WWII, the oil refineries of Ploesti, Romania, that was one of the bloodiest and costliest in WWII history.

Henry Lasko was one of the airmen who participated in the Ploesti Raids. Above left, Henry as a young airman, above in the center, Henry wounded, above right, Henry at the Ploesti Memorial, left, Henry with Cornell in Southern California.

I feel especially personal about this battle because I was, as a small boy, an eyewitness and survivor of the Ploesti Bombing Raids. I was with my father when he pulled some American crewmen out of a downed B24 Liberator. While I spent time hiding in the woods with the crewmen, they inspired me and that is when the love story started between America and me. I had an undying passion to get to this country, which I ultimately did when I escaped from the Communists in 1967. I made up my mind that I would never miss a chance to be here for the Veterans because they are the embodiment of what our country stands for and they are the protectors of our freedom.

They and their families suffered and died for us. Everything about the foundation will be for these Veterans. I have met the Veterans who were Prisoners of War in Romania and have heard their stories. Some even knew my dad. Our foundation would like to share the story of this battle and to honor those brave American airmen who sacrificed their lives for what they believed in: Freedom.

Our goal and my biggest dream have been as stated before,

to build a special memorial to those who made the ultimate sacrifice and never made it home. They are still to this day listed as Missing in Action. Their families had no real closure. I wanted to show respect and, in some way, pay back this country for the most precious gift of all - the gift of freedom!

This dream has been a long time coming. As far back as 18 years ago, the first rendering of the model for the bronze figures on the memorial was designed for me by producer, designer, and owner of Siteline in Costa Mesa, California, Gerry Rubin.

Things have progressed up to now. We have obtained the plot of land for the memorial, which was donated by Harbor Lawn-Mt Olive Memorial Park in Costa Mesa, California.

We have revised the original plans with new concepts for the appearance of the memorial thanks to Mr. Gerry Rubin and his enthusiastic support.

We have completed this book which will add to our fundraising efforts.

The special dream is becoming a reality and our heroes will not be forgotten.

www.ingramcontent.com/pod-product-compliance
Lightning Source LLC
LaVergne TN
LVHW051841080426
835512LV00018B/3000